A Monarch at Work

A Monarch at Work

The story of No 6024 *King Edward I*
on the mainline since 1990

Compiled by Tim Watson

Ian Allan
PUBLISHING

Contents

First published 2006

ISBN (10) 0 7110 3257 2
ISBN (13) 978 0 7110 3257 6

Published by the 6024 Preservation Society Ltd in association with Ian Allan Publishing Ltd, Hersham, Surrey KT12 4RG.

Printed by Ian Allan Printing Ltd, Hersham, Surrey KT12 4RG.

Front Cover: **26 October 2004** — Storming past Stoulton towards Evesham in evening light on the first long-haul special after the 2002-04 overhaul, to London from Worcester. *Phil Croutear*

Back Cover: King Edward I nameplate. *Mike Spencer*

Front endpaper: **10 January 1998** — Crossing the 20-arch Hoobrook viaduct at Kidderminster southwards on its way to Worcester and back to Didcot in bright winter sunshine with the 'Cathedrals Express'. *Mike Tyack*

Rear endpaper: **6 May 1991** — Sweeping down Hatton bank at sunset towards Banbury and Didcot, on the return run from Stratford-upon-Avon. *Dave Smith*

Half Title Page: **15 April 1990** — Running a shuttle between Tyseley and Stratford-upon-Avon at Earlswood. *Paul Stratford*

Title Page: **12 April 1993** — Running east of Newport before taking the 'North & West' route to Hereford, turning in Bulmers and then returning to Gloucester. *Dave Smith*

Left: **25 June 2005** — Kindly given access to parts of Old Oak Common depot by English Welsh & Scottish Railways, over 100 members and guests celebrate the 75th birthday of No 6024, posed here by the 'Factory'. *Tony Streeter/Steam Railway*

Preface

Most of the superb photographers who have contributed to this book will know well the frustrations of travelling miles to obtain one good shot of a main-line steam working hauled by No 6024 *King Edward I*. The sun may have gone in at the chosen location or it may be raining or smoke may be blowing over the side because of a change in the wind direction; all manner of difficulties.

With today's situation I feel privileged to have been able to see and photograph 'Kings' when they were working for their living in the hard times after the Second World War. I note on 25 July 1959 I spent a day near Reading — mostly in and around Sonning Cutting — watching the trains go by and taking over 80 photographs of what took my fancy and leaving out the other half! The worst part was the developing when I got home but that is another story. On that particular day I had 11 different 'Kings' before me, but sadly not No 6024, which may have gone up the Birmingham line for the day.

So what was special about the 'Kings' from a photographer's point of view? They generally hauled heavy trains and worked hard displaying a clean exhaust (unfortunately!) and looked superb when cleaned by a loving shed staff. Those engines which were not looked after often had inside cylinder glands leaking and the resultant steam coming through the frames could easily ruin the picture.

Living in the Midlands my favourite location was the climb out of Warwick to Hatton and the last few yards of the cutting coming under the three-arch bridge. The 09.10 Paddington-Birkenhead, on a still day, could be heard over two miles away and the adrenaline would be running high as it came round the corner (sun out ..... clean locomotive ..... shutter cocked?) and of course the sound was unique.

When the double-chimneys arrived in 1955 the sound changed to more of a roar and that is how it is today and long may it continue. With No 6024 having to be modified in order to comply with today's loading gauge it is not easy to find the correct angle at which the double-chimney is at its best. I know how I like things to be but would not wish to influence anyone else – the variables of railway photography are enormous.

The photographer today has a far more difficult task in his search for the master shot. No line-side access and the vegetation and tree-growth have made much of the railway impossible to use. This book is a splendid tribute to all the dedicated photographers whose work is reproduced here in all the different ways of interpretation.

Dick Blenkinsop

11 June 1957 — The 'King' reigning supreme and working for its living! Running at speed, No 6024 *King Edward I* passes Twyford on the down 'Bristolian' on a busy weekday, a few weeks before the visit described. *Dick Blenkinsop*

Acknowledgements

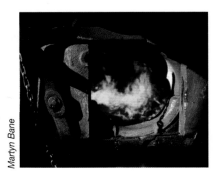

Martyn Bane

Fifteen years have passed since the publication of Chris Brown's excellent *A Monarch Restored*, which told the story of No 6024's antecedents, its production in 1930, its 32 years' work in the ownership of the Great Western and British Railways and its rapid demise in 1962. The difficult, complicated and lengthy transformation of the locomotive from a rusting carcass in 1973, to an active, viable machine in 1989 were described in great detail; the first tantalising moments of the locomotive where it belonged, working on the main-line concluded that part of the story on an optimistic note. So it's now time for another book to continue the story of No 6024's work to date (although for those who missed the first book, this one does provide a very brief *resumé* of the past history of the 'Kings' and of No 6024's restoration years).

Originally this was simply intended to be a collection of technically sound pictures recording *King Edward I's* life in traffic since 1990. It was going to represent faithfully as much of the engine's work as possible, using sharp, well-composed images to portray the different moods of the locomotive seen from the lineside or in the quiet and shadow of depots and sheds. But as the pictures came pouring in for possible inclusion, it became clear that this aim was rather modest and the finished product would achieve much more.

So we have managed both to collect expertly composed pictures of No 6024 which successfully show off its trademark immaculate appearance to best advantage and the power of its work; also unapologetically, the emphasis on the setting and the light is as important as the detail and work of the locomotive. We confess we have failed to represent every rail-tour and visit with a picture; rather, a number of shots of the same location or on the same date appear more than once simply because of the contrasting excellence of the pictures.

It could be argued that a key moment in the development of photography came when photographers perfected the skill of creating perfect still images of moving man-made objects, with railway trains the favoured subjects. Most of us with an interest in railways developed it through the medium of black and white pictures taken by a handful of inventive and enthusiastic experts and sharing their work was a crucial accessory to our passion. These photographers made the most of limited technology but were often trying to do something new. Then came colour transparencies — and we now have improving digital — accompanied by advanced techniques allowing truly superb reproduction. The importance of angles, shutter speed and exposure in classic locations has been matched by the desire to capture trains in majestic rural and urban landscapes, often involving magnificent railway structures and architecture, and making a

virtue out of necessity by exploiting the spectrum of light and dark and using the weather so the image is enhanced by the pristine qualities of sunshine and shade, or the glowering moodiness of an imminent storm.

As a result both colour and black and white pictures have been collected, each doing what they do best, demonstrating the photographers' skills in portraying this wonderful working machine. We thank with much appreciation Brian Bane, Martyn Bane, Andrew Bell, Terry Bennett, Don Bishop LRPS, Kevin Blake, Dick Blenkinsop, Huw Button, Matthew Carey, John Cooper-Smith, John Chalcraft/Rail Photoprints, Phil Croutear, Mike Dodd, Peter Doel, Tim Easter, Dave Fuszard, Brian Garrett, Bob Green, Mike Goodfield, David Holman, Nigel Hunt, Richard Jones, Richard Lewis, the late Graham Morgan, Geoff Plumb, Malcolm Ranieri, Dave Richards, Brian Robbins, Roger Siviter, Pete Skelton, Dave Smith, Mike Spencer, Paul Stratford, Tony Streeter/*Steam Railway* magazine, Eddie Sturgeon, Mike Tyack, Ralph Ward, Colin Washbourne, Phil Waterfield, Neville Wellings, John Whitehouse, John S. Whiteley, Michael Wild/*Steam Railway* magazine, Mark Wilkins, Nathan Williamson and Cliff Woodhead, all of whom donated their excellent work without charge.

Thanks are also due to Richard Abbey, Martyn Bane, Chris Brown, Dave Fuszard, Alan Lathey and Steve Underhill for their technical input. Richard Corser, Alan Lathey, Mike Notley, Alan Price, the late Brian Williams and Alastair Wood, who have recorded times and calculated power outputs for many years, provided the detailed data on the performances of the locomotive and we express our profound gratitude to them for the fruits of their extraordinary concentration.

Finally, our special thanks go to Dick Blenkinsop, photographer *par excellence* for over 50 years, who having been around the publishing block a few times, as well as donating his work, has provided invaluable advice, guidance and assistance to us in the selection of the pictures and the shaping of this book. His support over many years of 6024 Publications has been matchless.

Tim Watson

6

Introduction

Nigel Hunt

Background History

Most students of the history of the Great Western Railway trace the development of the four-cylinder 'King' class locomotive back to the early 20th century work of the Chief Mechanical Engineer (CME) of the Great Western, George Jackson Churchward. At the time, all railway companies were fiercely competitive and publicity conscious; locomotive design and technology were prime arenas for demonstrating ground-breaking creativity and technical excellence. During his time at Swindon, Churchward was constantly searching for improvements and innovations in his designs. Influenced first by American designs and later by French practice, his thinking evolved to favour six-coupled locomotives, with either two or four cylinders. Arguably, by the early 1920s the Great Western's two-cylinder and four-cylinder 4-6-0 designs were substantially superior to the locomotives of other railway companies.

Churchward's persuasion towards locomotives without trailing wheels was, for more than any other reason, a direct response to the need for maximum adhesion on the South Devon banks of Dainton, Rattery and Hemerdon on the West of England main line to Plymouth, then the Great Western's most important route. As a result, Swindon only ever produced one 'Pacific' (in 1907), No 111 *The Great Bear*, within which Churchward used many of the four-cylinder principals first developed in the 'Star' class, but after its limitations became clear, Churchward entirely lost interest in it, preferring instead to develop his ideas in locomotives without trailing-wheels. This limited his locomotives to narrow fireboxes and so he set out to ensure that his boiler designs benefited from good circulation. Combining relatively high boiler pressures with moderate levels of super-heat made efficient use of the high calorific-value steam coal which was readily available from the mines in South Wales.

In 1922 Churchward retired and his successor as CME, Charles Benjamin Collett, inherited a fine legacy of standardised Swindon designs. However, there was also a mixture of non-standard locomotives from the pre-Grouping railways at the Great Western's disposal and, as with the other 'Big Four' companies, Collett had the task of rationalising the fleet. In a climate of rising costs and falling income he also had to cope with catching up on the substantial under-investment which had occurred during and after World War 1. Collett, therefore, applied a pragmatic, economist's approach to the design of the Great Western's next generation of motive power. Seeing little wrong with Churchward's work he adapted and enlarged the earlier four-cylinder and two-cylinder designs, by developing the 'Castles' from the 'Stars' and the 'Halls' from the 'Saints'.

If there was a downside to this approach, it was the absence of much

2 July 1930 — Newly built, No 6024 (furthest from camera) stands alongside Nos 6022 and 6023 (also new), No 6020 (completed in April 1930) and Nos 6005, 6008 and 6017 (from the earlier 1927 batch). *Ian Allan Library*

British locomotive design). And F. W. Hawksworth, once he had succeeded Collett, incorporated some much-needed modernisation to the design of his 'County' class and the 'Modified Hall'. However, the whole strategy at the time was one of consolidation and rationalisation. Familiar with the traction they already possessed, they figured that if they didn't need to change things then there was no reason to do so.

Between June 1927 and July 1928 20 'Kings' were constructed in the first batch, to handle the heaviest of the principal expresses over the 'double-red' routes. By 1930, it became clear that the increased traffic demands justified the construction of another batch and 10 more were produced between May and July 1930. No 6024 *King Edward I* was completed in the second batch (Lot 267) on 30 June 1930, for a cost of £7,500 and was 'set to work' on 5 July 1930. It completed 237,871 miles before its first heavy overhaul in January 1935.

The locomotive was first allocated to Plymouth Laira and Newton Abbot, where it stayed until nationalisation in 1948, hauling the principal expresses between London and the West of England. In the nine-year period up to the outbreak of World War 2 it completed almost 500,000 miles and by nationalisation, almost 900,000 miles.

Horses for Courses

The history of the 'atmospheric' system in South Devon and the reasons for its ultimate failure are well-documented. In 1846 Brunel had been faced with the task of extending the railway to Plymouth in order to exploit its importance for the nation's defence and its siting as the first convenient land-fall on the eastern side of the Atlantic. Just as the London & South Western (L&SWR) did when it took the northerly route over Dartmoor to Plymouth (which, although climbing relentlessly both ways avoided the deep valleys of the Rivers Dart, Avon and Erme which flow off Dartmoor to the south coast), he had a number of choices in the route he could take. Continuing the policy of keeping the line as flat as previously achieved between London and Bristol and Bristol and Taunton, at first he followed the coast as far as possible. Solely taking note of topography, beyond Newton Abbot he might beneficially have gone as far as Torre and then strike inland towards the southwest of Totnes to avoid Dainton, before heading off towards Wrangaton at a lower level. In the other direction from Plymouth, the route might to advantage have gone via Yealmpton and Ermington rather than Plympton and Hemerdon, thus producing a line rather similar in character to the Midland Railway's 'Long Drag', involving longer but shallower gradients which would have been easier to operate than the route which was eventually built.

As it was, beyond Newton Abbot, he went inland across the hills and deep valleys which form the margins between the coast and the southern slopes of Dartmoor, possibly at the behest of the Admiralty which it was rumoured had national security concerns in view of the then-current hostile relations with France, but more probably in order to satisfy commercial obligations to those communities which were putting up the money for the railway. Inevitably this meant traction overcoming exceptionally steep and

advance on Churchward's original design concepts. By 1926 the demand for a locomotive still larger than the four-cylinder 'Castle' was becoming apparent and the CME was instructed by the Great Western General Manager, Sir Felix Pole, to proceed rapidly with the design and construction of a 'super-Castle', capable of hauling heavier passenger expresses on the Great Western between Paddington and Bristol, the West of England and the Midlands at average speeds around 60 mph. The 4-6-0 'King' class, which emerged from Swindon Works in June 1927, was a direct descendent of the 'Castle', but took on dimensions never previously seen in a 4-6-0 in the United Kingdom and represented the ultimate development of Churchward's four-cylinder concept. They were the heaviest (136 tons), and had the highest tractive effort (40,300lb) of any 4-6-0 locomotive ever to run in the United Kingdom. Their 22.5ton axle-loading restricted them to the Great Western and West of England main lines and the route to Wolverhampton, known as 'double-red' routes due to the Great Western's weight restriction code that appeared on the cab-sides of its locomotives. In the 1950s they also worked a limited service between Bristol and Shrewsbury through the Severn Tunnel.

However, apart from their size, in their basic design principles and detail the 'Kings' shared a close similarity with the 'Castles' and the 'Stars' of two decades previously. It wasn't that Swindon in the 1920s didn't possess the necessary skills to initiate design innovation any more. After all, W. A. Stanier took much Swindon practice to Crewe in 1932, and subsequently developed some of the finest locomotives the world was to see; (the 'Coronation' class was what many consider to be the ultimate in

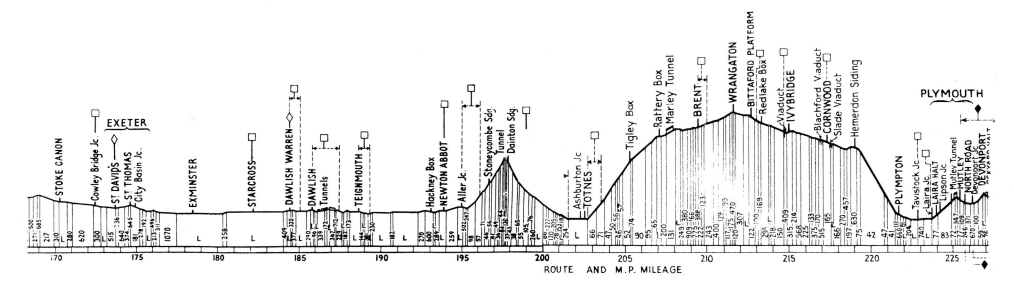

Above: Gradient profile between Exeter and Plymouth.

curvaceous inclines. With the existing motive power unsuitable, he started his use of an unconventional system already proven in Ireland and Croydon, south of London. However, after only two years in operation on the first section between Exeter and Newton Abbot, the 'atmospheric' concept was abandoned entirely, let down by the technology of the day and its incompatibility with the remainder of the network and rolling stock. Thus, generations of operations' planners and footplate crews were left with the permanent legacy of working the intense West of England traffic with conventional locomotives over short but exceptionally steep gradients. As a result, to the end of steam, Swindon's designers and engineers had this stretch of main-line railway in mind when evolving their locomotive designs.

Going westwards, the first of these climbs, to Dainton tunnel, starts only a few feet above sea level, less than a mile and a half out of Newton Abbot, so a beneficial high-speed approach to the bank is impossible. Though climbing for only two miles, the line, doing its best to follow the most favourable route the contours allow, twists and turns its way past Stoneycombe Quarry at gradients ranging from 1 in 98 to 1 in 36 to the summit's 'hump' just beyond Dainton Tunnel at MP218, which is almost 250ft above sea level, before falling away at 1 in 37 the other side. Particularly here, the firemen had to keep a close eye on the boiler water-level inside the tunnel because of the rapid change in the locomotive's inclination as it topped the summit. However, it is the sinuous nature of the alignment combined with the constantly varying gradients which makes Dainton bank westbound so challenging in avoiding wheel-slip.

From the summit the line drops steeply at first, through another series of curves which limit the line-speed, to a mile-length level section at Totnes, again just feet above sea level. Immediately after Totnes station, the line starts a continuous climb for nine miles, the first three miles to the site of Tigley box at gradients of 1 in 66/71 increasing to 1 in 47/52, punctuated by short sections of 1 in 50/56/46 and 57. At Tigley the gradient eases to 1 in 90/95 and 1 in 65 for the next two miles, to Rattery. Here, with his fire in good shape, the fireman could put his shovel down and reflect on a good day's work. The climb is further eased to the summit at Wrangaton (MP232) which is over 450ft above sea level on the southern edge of Dartmoor.

From Wrangaton the line now gradually falls for seven miles to the site of Hemerdon sidings where the tracks dramatically plummet down for two and a quarter miles at the alarming inclination of 1 in 42/47/41. With the line almost dead straight heavy braking was required to avoid excessive speeds that would otherwise cause great embarrassment if the Plympton 'distant' signal was at caution and the subsequent 'home' was at danger. Apart from a short but sharp rise from Laira to Mutley tunnel, the locomotive's work was done and Plymouth North Road was reached almost immediately after the tunnel. Thus ends possibly the most exciting and exacting 52 miles (from Exeter) of main line in the country. The contrast between the stretches along the coast and the Teign estuary and the steep ascending and descending sections deep in Devon's valleys and on the tops skirting Dartmoor take the breath away for their scenic interest, not to mention the effort required by crew and machine.

From 1927, 'Kings' were limited to 360 tons (10 GWR vehicles, nine BR Mark 1s) unassisted, 'Castles' to 315 tons and 'Stars' to 288 tons over

9

these banks. The objective was that, come rain or shine, any member of the class should be able to keep its train moving to time, or if forced to stop or if checked for any reason, it should be able to restart its train on any part of the banks without calling for assistance. When these load-limits were arrived at, it was the all-important non-stop traffic from Plymouth to London which was critical. Cold locomotives starting from Plymouth arrived at Hemerdon bank's two and a quarter miles after only four miles work from North Road. Moreover, prewar, there was the additional handicap of speed restrictions of 40mph at Laira Junction and, just a mile from the foot of the bank, 45mph at Tavistock Junction. It was essential that every locomotive should be able to cope with Hemerdon without losing time, even if it was actually held by signals at the bottom or on the gradient itself.

Michael Rutherford's fine technical study *'Castles' & 'Kings' at Work* records that in 1922 (prior to the introduction of the first 'Castle') a paper was presented to the Engineering Society on the subject of Great Western locomotive 'Proportion and Performance' and the relevant section focused specifically on footplate practice when climbing Hemerdon bank. It had been found that 90% of the maximum available effort of the example engine — a 'Star'— was required to keep its permitted load moving and take it over the summit. It was also found on a number of occasions that 100% of the maximum available effort was required after a signal stop or check. 'Maximum' was described as full regulator in full gear. In this context the paper emphasised that slipping was 'a type of set-back which cannot again be fully recovered'. The natural transference of weight from the bogie to the rear driving wheels on starting locomotives meant that there was less of a risk of losing adhesion with a 4-4-0, 4-6-0 or a 2-8-0 than with 4-4-2s, 2-6-2s or 4-6-2s without compensated suspension, and was thus the reason for the Great Western's preference for locomotives without trailing wheels. Significantly, records indicate that *The Great Bear* never made it to Plymouth in traffic as it would have spread the track too much on the curves.

The experiences with 4-4-2s had resulted in the construction of the first 4-6-0 for comparison purposes (in 1902), a two-cylinder locomotive No 100; in 1905 the first four-cylinder locomotives appeared. Churchward eventually concluded that for express passenger work the four-cylinder 4-6-0s were best, their increased adhesion allowing the haulage of heavier loads without loss of time and the smoothness provided by their divided-drive reducing wear and allowing higher mileages between overhauls. In Collett's time it was the need to take higher tonnages over the South Devon banks which prompted the introduction of the 'Castles' and then the 'Kings', the 'Stars' having already proved themselves capable of hauling prodigious loads over the rest of the Great Western network. So it was, that Swindon pragmatically favoured passenger and freight locomotives alike with good factors of adhesion and high tractive effort, capable of short but fierce bursts of sure-footed high power output, consciously forsaking the benefits of wide fireboxes for good adhesion.

Theoretically, the 'Star' was the only Great Western four-cylinder 4-6-0 that could be driven with full regulator in full gear without losing its feet.

Dave Fuszard

The load limits for both the 'Castles' and 'Kings' were not *pro rata* to the increase in tractive effort, due to the reduction in adhesion factor. It ought not to have been possible to drive a 'King' on full regulator in full gear without slipping, but in practice, there was little point in working a 'King' like that much above 10mph anyway, as the volumes of steam could not be exhausted efficiently. However, it does indicate that if pushed the 'Kings' could have managed 400 tons over the banks; reports exist of 'Kings' handling loads heavier than 360 tons.

In addition, the 1922 paper promoted the introduction of the screw-reverser in preference to the reversing 'lever', it being a better method of feeding in gradual changes to the cut-off, stating that '.....any other method a momentary acceleration is introduced that produces slipping ..... to reduce any variables whilst negotiating the bank, the necessary regulator opening is gradually obtained before altering or increasing the cut-off position'. Therefore, at all costs, the attention of engineers and crews was concentrated on avoiding even a single slip which may fatally affect the timetable. In an article in May 1957's edition of *Trains Illustrated*, the late Cecil J. Allen wrote about the South Devon banks '....With gradients of such severity a single coach more or less will affect the climbing speeds considerably. Locomotive handling of the most expert description is an indispensable requirement; an increase in cut-off delayed by, perhaps, no more than half-a-mile, may make all the difference between a successful climb and something not far removed from stalling. Given a reasonably full boiler and a good head of steam, however, none of these climbs is long enough to give anxiety about water level or pressure; the prime consideration is simply to keep moving'.

Swindon, from the days of its earliest six-coupled locomotives, decided that it was willing to forfeit wide-fireboxes (and thus the potential for loco-

6024 Archives

Opposite page: **29 January 2005 —** Storming Dainton bank westbound with a maximum load on the approach to the tunnel, on a special from Bristol to Plymouth and return. *Terry Bennett*

motives capable of generating significantly higher draw-bar horsepower), in the interest of operating locomotives with good adhesion. As a consequence the 'King', with all its dimensions designed at about the limit that a 4-6-0 chassis could handle, was equipped with the largest possible taper-boiler combined with a long but relatively small firebox. This well-suited the 1920s Great Western practice for the 'Limited'; leaving Paddington with a 500-ton load, by the time it had reached Newton Abbot, the load would have reduced to 360 tons by regularly 'slipping' its coaches, with the boiler and firebox having a consistent demand on them as the journey progressed and the severity of the road increased. Other principal trains reduced their loads by stopping at Exeter or Newton Abbot to detach portions for Torbay. This was a carefully considered approach, vindicated by the continued success of the design after modification through the 1950s and even today well-justified judging by some of No 6024's sensational performances on home territory. When required, No 6024 has demonstrated it is capable of producing exceptionally high steaming rates and outputs of power with heavy trains over hilly routes at high average speeds.

During the 1948 Locomotive Exchanges, the load limits to Plymouth were strictly adhered to and the outcome convinced both Swindon and Paddington that in day-to-day use the more powerful SR, LMS and LNER Pacifics had no significant advantage over the Great Western's 4-6-0s. The

Exchanges demonstrated that the Pacifics' extra power could not practicably be translated into faster climbing or haulage of heavier loads, due to their lower Adhesion Factor and the increased risk of slipping. The BR Standard 7P 'Britannia' class Pacifics allocated to the southwest in the early 1950s, on a day in, day out evaluation were capable of only loading to the equivalent of a 'Castle' and were eventually evicted from the southwest by the Divisional Civil Engineer as they were spreading the track too much on the curves. Comfortable in adhering to Great Western practice, Paddington approved the modifications carried out to the 'Kings', confident that the Swindon 4-6-0 designs were still the answer. When the Western Region had LMR Pacifics on loan in the mid-1950s the limit was one coach less and not exceeded without assistance.

A recent study explaining the background of the rumoured Swindon 4-6-2 (under Hawksworth in the late 1940s), argued that if there had been the need to develop a bigger locomotive than the 'King', then Swindon almost certainly would have preferred a 4-8-0 express locomotive rather than a Pacific, primarily to achieve satisfactory adhesion on the banks. Undoubtedly a 4-8-0 would have been more secure climbing with heavier loads than a Pacific and could have achieved very high power outputs judging by the French experience with 4-8-0s. Whether or not the crews would have managed the inevitably longer firebox is open to conjecture and no doubt the longer wheel-base would also have damaged the track.

Driving and Firing

Even if the 'King' is driven efficiently its front-end can beat the boiler. It has valve and cylinder dimensions similar to the 'Duchess' but a boiler considerably smaller and a grate area only two-thirds the size of Stanier's Pacifics. When working hard the 'King' can burn coal faster than the fireman can replace it, hence the need for the fireman to anticipate the demands for steam and keep a good fire. However, for all practical purposes, the grate is about as big as a narrow firebox can accommodate, the limit on its width due to the 4-6-0 wheel arrangement making it disproportionately small to the boiler's capacity. Churchward's designs had paid particular attention to water circulation and so, despite the relatively small area of the grate, the 'King' boiler/firebox combination works perfectly adequately because many of the long climbs on western lines such as Savernake, Whiteball, Wellington, Brewham, Church Stretton and Sapperton are characterised by several miles of gentle slopes leading to three of four miles of very steep gradients. The 'Kings' were designed to achieve optimum combustion rates at 45 to 55mph on the lower slopes when hauling big trains and briefly develop very high evaporation rates which, although only sustainable for short periods, would deal with the short but severe gradients before the summit. Fast running down the other side, under light steam while refilling the boiler and reviving steam pressure was normal.

The class's principal Achilles' heel, compared with more recent designs, is the arrangement of its exhaust steam passages. Based on the 'Stars', which had much less volumes of steam to handle, the exhaust ports of a 'King' are incapable of dealing with the quantity of exhaust steam pro-

2 July 2005 — Powering past Kintbury at the start of the 10-mile climb to Savernake with the '75th Anniversary Limited', a special charter, which ran from London Paddington to Kingswear, to celebrate the locomotive's 75th birthday. *Richard Lewis*

duced when travelling at speed with wide regulator openings on short cut-offs. The resulting cylinder back pressure is noticeably telling when working hard at speeds much above 60mph, particularly uphill. This was one of the first things Stanier tackled on the LMS and the reason why the 'Duchess' has the capacity to keep delivering rapid acceleration well above 60mph. Swindon also looked at 'streamlining' the internal passages on the 'Kings' in the 1950s, when new front-ends and cylinders were fitted, and would have pursued it but for the space limitations between the frames which precluded a cost-effective modification. It is also debatable whether or not the original chassis would have been capable of withstanding the increased stresses brought about by the substantially larger power outputs that would have resulted. An opposing view is that the increased efficiency resulting in much reduced back-pressure would actually have decreased the impact on the frames. Instead, with time short, Swindon went for much cheaper smokebox modifications. These improved the running freedom of the locomotives considerably, but did not deal with the fundamental design limitations.

So, to overcome at least partially some of these design shortcomings, driving technique is important and considerable *finesse* is needed. Long periods of full regulator with a long cut-off after accelerating away from a start will increase cylinder back-pressure and can badly deplete the boiler. A better result is produced by partially opening the regulator in the main valve and gradually adjusting the reverser setting until the train has reached a good pace. On typical undulating Western routes, working with the regulator main valve just cracked open, combined with a slightly longer cut-off at first will deliver optimum steam expansion and exhaust efficiency and reach the necessary road speed after good acceleration; then speed is maintained by making subtle adjustments of the reverser, rather than to the regulator, to suit the road. Only on the severest climbs and only for relatively short periods would the regulator be fully opened.

The remarkable Kenneth H. Leech, in his collaboration *Portrait of 'Kings'* with Bryan Holden, describes the different handling by drivers and firemen he observed on the footplate. He recalls in particular 'Driver Walter Harris, a great character and a first-class engineman who, when working between Newton Abbot and Plymouth on the down "10.30 Limited" was continually altering the setting of the reversing lever to suit the road. Up the steep banks of Dainton and Rattery he would work the engine at 40-45% cut-off, dropping down to 15% on the easy portions of the road. But when he shut off going down banks, or because of a curve ahead with perhaps a 50 mph. limit, the reversing lever would be dropped into its 'rolling' position of 45%. Driver Harris's mates thought him one of the greatest drivers on the Great Western. He certainly saved the company a good deal of coal!'. This technique would be more the norm. On the other hand, another of Kenneth's driver friends working the same load over the exact route 'would simply set the reversing lever in 40% and give the engine full regulator up the banks, pull it back into first port on the level and shut it off downhill. Always the (reversing) lever was notched

Richard Jones

up at 40%. The driver simply altered the regulator from full open to completely shut according to the gradient and the circumstances. He may have saved himself trouble, but he was not popular with his fireman!' It should be added that on normally graded routes, it was uncommon to work a 'King' on cut-offs exceeding 25% other than starting or recovering from checks. One driver related that, with a moderate load, you could get from Newton Abbot to Paddington on 15%!

As with driving, firing a 'King' needs great skill. Particularly for an inexperienced fireman, the firebox at 11ft 6in in length is about as intimidating as it can get. The grate is divided into three sections: the front and middle slope towards the tube-plate (over which the inclined brick-arch hangs); the back section is horizontal, about 18in below the fire-hole. The ideal is to have an even level of fire the full length, about a foot thick parallel with the sloping grate and continuing to thicken towards the bottom edge of the fire-hole and in the back corners. After making a good fire, the basics, such as shovelling 'little and often' apply, but getting coal down to the front is crucial to maintaining the temperature of the brick-arch. Too much fire at the back risks the fireman's shovel directing coal upwards and so forming a 'hump' in the middle where the brick-arch starts. Then, fire-

irons have to be deployed to disperse the hump and level things off. A falling boiler pressure gauge is a sure sign that the brick-arch has cooled, due to insufficient heat at the front.

The supply of a steady and consistent draught through the back damper door under the grate combined with a small amount of secondary air past the flap would be the usual circumstances for long-distance non-stop working and would generally keep the fire in good shape, provided the fireman's technique was adapted to the demands of the locomotive. It was fairly common, however, that well into his journey, the fireman would have to knock the fire around to liven it up. In the days when fuel economy was an important part of the job, over-firing was uncommon. These days, some firemen, fearful of losing pressure, will over-fire and the outcome can be self-fulfilling. There is only so much coal the grate can burn at one time and the natural tendency to pile on more coal when pressure is dropping will end unhappily, with unburned coal or clinker accumulating on the grate and vast quantities of semi-burned char amassing in the smokebox, eventually to interfere with the draughting.

Equally, judging the level of water in the boiler to suit circumstances is crucial. 'Mortgaging' the boiler when climbing — the art of maintaining steam pressure at the expense of a falling water level — was a common device if the locomotive was struggling for steam, as Western firemen knew that relief would shortly arrive at the summit of the bank. The use of an exhaust injector allowed accurate adjustment of water-flow into the boiler, with the live injector used less frequently. The fireman's unique skill was having a knowledge of the required water level at any location and could be the difference between running on time and arriving late.

Kenneth Leech exclaimed that 'firing a "King" was a man's job'. This was because these engines burned more coal in the front of the firebox than they did under the firehole, which meant that the fireman did not follow the usual Great Western practice of packing coal right up to or above firehole level, into the corners, leaving the fire thin at the front. When firing a double-chimney 'King', the greater part of the coal had to be thrown the full length of the firebox, a distance of over 11 feet, preferably right to the front, so that it actually knocked on the tube plate.

It should not be overlooked that crews working between Paddington and Plymouth were unrelieved and thus, in terrain, distance and time had the longest and toughest turns of any crews in the country. This could be over seven hours if the schedule was via Bristol.

Postwar developments and on British Railways

After nationalisation, British Railways carried out the Locomotive Exchanges to assess the existing national locomotive fleet prior to embarking on the designs of the proposed 'Standard' classes of locomotives. No 6018 *King Henry VI* was selected to take part but, due to gauging problems, could only work on the Eastern Region, out of King's Cross. The locomotive performed competently but supplied with 'hard' northern coal exhibited inferior fuel performance compared with the more modern, higher super-heat designs in its test group. Swindon had already experimentally modified No 6022 *King*

Edward III with higher super-heat, so with future supplies of high-calorific Welsh coal uncertain decided to fit the entire class with new boilers with four-row super-heaters. The modification of all 30 locomotives was completed by the mid-1950s, No 6024 receiving its first four-row super-heater boiler in September 1953 when the engine had completed over 1,000,000 miles in service. The improvements in steam generation resulted in the potential for much higher steaming rates.

Following trials with several installations of 'self-cleaning' arrangements for spark-arresting in smokeboxes, Swindon sought to improve the smokebox vacuum by experimenting with the draughting. Tests showed that higher steaming rates could be realised but the original smokebox design plus the resistance exerted on gas-flow by spark screens hampered the full utilisation of this extra capability. Further trial modifications to the smoke-box and chimney were carried out which after some interim snags eventually culminated in the fitting of double blast-pipes and a double-chimney to No 6015 *King Richard III*, with startling results. The entire class was eventually modified and proved that not only were they able to live up to their long-held reputation for handling heavy loads, but compared with the original locomotives they gained greater freedom from mechanical resistance, allowing high-speed running with speeds regularly over 90mph and occasionally in excess of 100mph. Revitalised, the 'Kings' were able to cope with the Western Region's accelerated schedules with ease, generally having plenty of power in hand and they retained their position as the region's premier motive power on all the major routes until finally superseded by diesel-hydraulics.

In common with the entire class No 6024 was fitted with new cylinders and, in November 1957, with double blast-pipe modifications and the final design of double-chimney. In March 1960, it was fitted with the boiler it still carries (boiler No 8610, fitted new to No 6027 in 1953 and carried previously by Nos 6018 and 6000). In just over two years up to withdrawal, the locomotive ran 94,384 miles with this boiler.

King Edward I ran for over 30 years on the Great Western Railway and the Western Region of British Railways, regularly hauling express passenger services such as the 'Cornish Riviera Express', 'The Bristolian', the 'Inter City' and the 'Cambrian Coast Express'. It worked a total of 1,570,015 miles and was a member of that *elite* group of 'Kings' which recorded speeds of 100mph or more on a number of occasions. In BR days the locomotive was allocated to Plymouth Laira, Old Oak Common and finally Cardiff Canton, when in the early 1960s the long-standing restrictions for the class were relaxed to allow 'Kings' as far as Cardiff.

The class's longevity became legendary, demonstrated by the locomotives' domination of the principal Great Western and British Railways services from the late 1920s to the early 1960s. Unlike many classes, right to the end of their working lives the 'Kings' avoided the ignominy of being consigned to minor duties, instead handling the most important traffic between London and the Midlands and South Wales. It was, however, with ruthless disregard for their individual condition that the entire class was abruptly and prematurely withdrawn from service in 1962 as diesels

Martyn Bane

Opposite page: **5 February 1995** — Looking almost timeless storming through Goring & Streatley on a damp, foggy morning, on its way to Bristol and Paignton from Paddington. *Dick Blenkinsop*

replaced them on the double-red routes. No 6006 went in February 1962 and the remainder between June and December 1962. No 6018 *King Henry VI* reappeared in 1963 on a Stephenson Locomotive Society special and, going out with a flourish, touched 96mph at Denham. The continuation of steam on the WR for a while afterwards suggests that at least some examples of the class could have gone on bit longer. All but Nos 6000, 6023 and 6024 were scrapped.

Withdrawal and Restoration

Withdrawn from BR service at the end of June 1962 (with No 6023 *King Edward II*) No 6024 languished at Swindon for a while before being sold for scrapping to Wards of Briton Ferry. Axle-weight restrictions prevented its movement beyond Cardiff and it was eventually resold to Woodham

Brothers and it ended up on Barry Island for scrapping. With No 6023, it gently rotted in the company of over 200 other locomotives while the cutting torches focused on the easier, more lucrative railway wagons.

Inspired by preserved class-mate No 6000 *King George V's* 1971 breach of BR's steam ban, the 'King Preservation Society' bought No 6024 for around £4,000 in 1973, with the purpose of restoring it to main-line condition. With many components missing, including its double-chimney (currently fitted to No 6000, now located at the Steam Museum, Swindon), and with piston, connecting and eccentric rods and slide-bars cut through, at the time the project had all the appearances of a 'mission impossible'. Both Nos 6023 and 6024 were available but No 6024 was the better option, because after a derailment in the Barry yard No 6023 had had its rear driving wheels torched through and at the time was con-

30 October 1992 — As-restored — on display inside the shed at the Great Western Society, Didcot shed during a photographic evening.
Colin Washbourne

sidered beyond repair. No 6023 is now being rebuilt in single-chimney form at the Great Western Society, Didcot.

In 1974, the 36th locomotive to be rescued from Barry, No 6024 was moved to the Buckinghamshire Railway Centre at Quainton Road, and the Society made slow but steady progress towards the restoration of the locomotive. In 1981, the renamed '6024 Preservation Society Ltd' introduced a new funding initiative, the *Club 100*, which in crucial ways proved the project's turning-point and by 1984 was fully subscribed. The revenue generated by the *Club 100*, and its successor *Club Sixty-Twenty Four*, enabled progress to accelerate and has become the highly successful financial foundation for all of the Society's activities. The restoration at Quainton Road by Society members took 16 years — for the first 12 in the open air — but it was worth it. The locomotive emerged painted in

Great Western livery and on 2 February 1989, No 6024 moved again under its own power and amidst considerable public interest and media coverage was recommissioned on 26 April 1989 by HRH the Duke of Gloucester. In October 1989 it was moved by road from Quainton to the Birmingham Railway Museum (now the Tyseley Locomotive Works), from where it completed its main-line test runs. On 15 April 1990, it resumed its main-line career hauling revenue-earning passenger trains.

In recognition of the high standard to which the locomotive had been restored, No 6024 was outright winner of the 1990 British Coal-sponsored Heritage Award (for a restoration project) and awarded the £3,000 prize which was put towards the purchase and restoration of an ex-British Rail Mark 1 BSK coach, for transporting support crew and equipment for main-line work.

essary funds too demanding. Loadings have tended to get heavier and apart from 1993, year on year the engine has worked increasingly greater mileages. 'Open access' of the national network brought more routes into play in early 1992 and No 6024 was increasingly seen hauling passenger charter trains on a number of previously banned routes, including the main lines to the West of England via Bristol and to South Wales, through the Severn Tunnel.

Fitted with BR's standard Automatic Warning System (AWS) permitting speeds up to 75mph, No 6024 reintroduced steam-hauled express passenger trains to a number of new destinations within western zones for the first time for some years, including Cardiff, Bristol Temple Meads, Gloucester, Exeter, Swansea, Worcester, Newton Abbot and Paignton. In August 1992 the locomotive made its promised return to Quainton Road, this time via the main line, where in the company of 'Castle' class No 5029 *Nunney Castle*, it hauled shuttles to and from Aylesbury.

In March 1995, after over five years activity in main-line traffic and seven years from when the 'King' was granted its first boiler ticket, the locomotive passed into the night and withdrew from traffic for its heavy overhaul, working on British Rail metals for the last time. Since its main-line reappearance in 1990, the engine had handled 42 rail-tours, running almost 10,000 main-line miles. Twenty-three of these trains (55%) were formed of 12 Mark 1 coaches (about 480 tons). No 6024 retired to a secure MoD site at BAD Kineton in Warwickshire for the Society to carry out the overhaul. Remarkably, its driving wheel tyres, close to scrapping thickness when the locomotive was rescued from Barry, had sustained so little wear that they were considered good for the next period on the main line.

Above: **16 August 1991** — Turning at Old Oak Common, with (left to right) No 3440 *City of Truro*, No 6998 *Burton Agnes Hall* and No 5029 *Nunney Castle* in the background.
Colin Washbourne

Right: **4 January 2003** — Withdrawn for overhaul and awaiting major dismantling to start at Tyseley Locomotive Works.
Dave Fuszard

1990 to 1995, overhaul and back to the privatised railway

The Society was invited by BR to provide No 6024 to haul the *InterCity* VIP special on 19 May 1990. In July 1990 the locomotive appeared at the National Railway Museum's *Exhibition On Tour*, held at Swindon Works, where the locomotive's 60th anniversary was celebrated, stabled alongside classmate No 6000 *King George V*.

The locomotive rapidly became a favourite main-line performer. At first, based either at Tyseley or Didcot, it repeatedly put on exhilarating performances in its expanding main-line programme, hauling trains to Derby, Birmingham, Stratford upon Avon, Swindon, Newport, Shrewsbury and Chester. With increased regularity the locomotive was calculated to be achieving extraordinary drawbar horsepower outputs but although it got close a number of times, the magic 2,000 eluded the locomotive. In 1991 the locomotive hauled rail-tours from London Paddington, its first appearance there for almost 30 years.

No 6024's first period back on the main line coincided with the railway industry preparing for privatisation. The steam charter market was expanding and more locomotives were emerging from restoration for the first time; and there was a proliferation of promoters. Many of the locomotives originally inherited from BR retired for their first full overhauls and some have not returned so far as owners have found raising the nec-

The 'King' was fitted with a number of small but significant modifications, incorporated in order to increase its availability. The modifications included the fitting of dual-braking equipment (air and vacuum) to increase flexibility in the use of different rakes of passenger stock. The air-pump is discreetly fitted within the locomotive's frames, but regrettably the system's reliability has been questionable, and remains so to this day. An experimental modification was also carried out, with new blast-pipes with slightly larger nozzles being fitted. The aim was to slightly soften the blast as the view was that after restoration when the locomotive was fitted with two live steam injectors (rather than one live steam and one exhaust injector as in Great Western and BR days) the blast was sharper because greater volumes of exhaust steam had to pass through the nozzles. Particularly at high steaming rates it was possible to 'overload' the nozzles, running the risk of causing too much draught and eventually 'choking' the blast-pipes causing excessive back-pressure in the cylinders. In cases of sustained very hard working, it was considered that the nozzles could also reach 'sonic' flow, which places an upper limit on blast-pipe performance and drastically reduces draughting efficiency.

The other modification was the reduction of No 6024's chimney, safety valves and cab-roof heights to get it to fit within the standard height of 13ft 1in. This allowed it to make its long-awaited but triumphant return to Plymouth, first double-headed in November 1996; and then in April 1997 it ran solo, the first time an unassisted steam locomotive had been entrusted with a passenger train over the route to Plymouth since the early 1960s. The locomotive also achieved a number of other 'firsts', stemming from 'open access' and these modifications, although when first decided upon the Society was only aiming to return to the Western lines it had previously been barred from because of its height.

In September 1996 the locomotive returned to the new privatised railway owned by Railtrack. Perhaps fortuitously, this period of absence allowed the railway industry to settle down under the new arrangements. Although many senior railwaymen had retired and their skills would never again be employed on footplates on the main line, the promised routes had become available and the new arrangements allowed fresh steam men to emerge. There were noticeably different attitudes apparent straightaway, with footplate crews displaying greater enthusiasm for the steam jobs and being more willing to both teach and learn; much of the previous culture had evaporated. Although some of the new men lacked the depth of experience gained in BR steam days, these crews have been quick learners and over the years have delivered some unforgettable runs on the 'King'.

Height Modifications

In March 1992 the locomotive's safety-valves had hit the over-bridge over the Great Western main line at Ladbroke Grove and although this was a BR Civil Engineering error, the Society was thereafter always sensitive to the height of the locomotive and constantly aware of gauging difficulties. This sensitivity was increased when 'open access' began to lead to a substantial expansion of the scope of main-line steam. Advice at the time was

clear, that the locomotive's height of 13ft 5in would make it increasingly difficult for civil engineers and gauging engineers to clear No 6024 for most of the new routes — particularly 'under the wires' — and therefore the Society was faced with the irony of the prospect of an increased number of steam routes becoming available, with fewer and fewer — including Paddington itself — accessible to the 'King'.

This was brought home, when, in late 1994, the Society planned to take the locomotive to Plymouth. Having attracted a promoter the proposal was thwarted at the 11th hour by the decision that the loco could get to Plymouth, but could not get back! The 'shoulders' of the cab-roof would foul the skew overbridge at Plympton at the foot of Hemerdon bank. Earlier that year, after the Exeter Rail Fair, the engine had run light with support coach down to the Paignton & Dartmouth Steam Railway and had had to return 'wrong-line' from Paignton because of an over-bridge at Torre. The same answer was proposed for the situation at Plympton, but unsurprisingly the authorities would not accept this.

With the first overhaul looming in early 1995, the Society had decided to undertake a study of the critical heights to assess the potential for reduction; these were the cab-roof, the whistles, the safety-valves and their brass bonnet and the chimney. The result of the studies was positive in all four areas and eventually the modified locomotive re-emerged in September 1996. The Society went to great lengths to consult with its

22 March 1992 — After returning from Stratford-upon-Avon, in Paddington's Platform No 1 minus its safety valves, having caught a steel girder on the underside of the over-bridge at Ladbroke Grove while running on the Up Main. This event started the process which led to the locomotive's height being reduced at the safety valves, chimney and cab. *Dave Fuszard*

members on the proposals and also to prepare the wider public for what was anticipated would be a controversial change. Happily, the response was almost universally positive.

As well as being far from an aesthetic disaster, operationally the Society was completely satisfied that this was the right thing to do, and took the view that, just as Swindon modified the entire class to keep up with changing conditions in the 1950s, so it was necessary to adopt a similar attitude in order to operate within an ever-changing railway environment in the 1990s. This approach justified itself entirely, because within two months after its return, the locomotive had made its triumphant return to Plymouth out of Paddington (under the wires), and subsequently found itself in many locations previously unavailable to it.

1996 to 2002

The modifications to the height produced opportunities never expected. As well as returning to many traditional Western locations on its old core routes previously denied it, No 6024 was able to haul trains on many of the national network's other major routes, some of which are under the 25kV wires. Now authentically painted in the final British Railways livery it had carried to its demise in 1962, the locomotive appeared at the London termini of King's Cross and Victoria, as well as Paddington and the engine has been seen at points as far-flung as Penzance, Falmouth, Par, Carmarthen, Fishguard, Crewe, Holyhead, Preston, Carlisle, Blackburn, York, Leeds, Doncaster, Peterborough, Norwich, Cambridge, Salisbury,

Bournemouth, Weymouth. Apart from during the 1948 Exchanges none of these destinations saw 'Kings' in Great Western or British Railways days as gauging and weight limitations restricted them to their core routes.

However, it wasn't all easy. In 1996 commercial demands were requiring heavier loads than ever before and although it appeared that the 13-coach load on the first handful of rail-tours reflected the understandable interest in the locomotive, 500-plus tons on the drawbar became the rule rather than the exception, a contrast with the period up to 1995. It emerged that an uninformed notion was prevailing amongst decision-makers that the locomotive's British Railways '8P' classification automatically made it the equal of all other '8P' locomotives, no matter where it was running. There appeared to be no understanding that its classification, while fully justified on Western routes, was entirely untried elsewhere and it would take more than a miracle for the locomotive — with its narrow grate of 34sq ft — to match the power outputs of more modern locomotives with much larger square grates, with these loads. Many observers at the time wrote off the locomotive after its work in the North of England, as inferior in all circumstances. This underlines the inadequacy of a power classification based on tractive effort.

Unfortunately, following its return to traffic, the locomotive did have a period when its steaming was unreliable, which didn't help matters. A number of commentators put this down directly to the reduction in height, asserting that the modification to the chimney had caused interference to the draughting. The facts, however, were different, as there had been no alteration to the critical dimensions or the relationship between the blast-pipes and the chimney orifices. Others argued that the experimental blast-pipes had altered the set-up. At the outset these had been quickly replaced with the originals in order to remove any question of this, and only reinstated once the steaming problems had been overcome. However, periods of poor steaming were a concern as such incidents had been rare during the first boiler ticket and had become far more frequent in the second.

It was eventually worked out that there were a number of contributors to this. One feature was simply the new crews' lack of familiarity with the locomotive and its use on routes for which it was less suited. Another was the unusually increased loads consistently being required, particularly on routes less suited to the locomotive. Also, work under the 25kV wires didn't suit the engine as the wires prevented the use of the locomotive's long fire-irons whose regular use is essential to keep the fire clean. Unfortunately, there are also wide variables in the quality of coal available and its characteristics, which occasionally caused a less than sparkling performance. Crucially, however, it became plain after a number of runs demanding sustained evaporation rates that the smokebox door had been leaking unnoticed.

Other obstacles appeared. Railtrack's local management in charge of the new territories unused to steam were experiencing a range of problems not seen for a generation. A handful of line-side fire incidents up to 1997 caused problems to signalling infrastructure and, by early 1998, two-stage spark-arresting became mandatory. No 6024 was already equipped with a

Far right: **14 March 1998** — Leaving Appleby southbound in angry-looking light on its first encounter with the S&C from Carlisle. *John S. Whiteley*

Below: **19 September 1998** — Arrival at Penzance, the first ever by a 'King', after a lively run. *Dave Fuszard*

mesh cage around the blast-pipes and double-chimney petticoats, as fitted in the final form of the smokebox.

In the late 1950s various spark-arresting systems were tried which were termed 'self-cleaning' that is, all but the largest particles of coal and char drawn into the smokebox would be expelled through the chimney. During trials, Swindon had experimented with a number of arrangements. Solid plates angled between the top of the tube-plate and the blast-pipes were tried, against which the particles impacted before disintegrating and being expelled; another method was the fitting of vertical mesh screens the full height of the tubed area just ahead of the tube-plate, to catch the largest particles which would then accumulate on the floor of the smoke-box. These ultimately were replaced by the final arrangement because the screens more often than not ended up on the depot floor rather than in the smoke-box because their removal and replacement was such a hassle. No 6024's new arrangements fitted in 1998 were a combination of the existing cage plus a vertical mesh screen ahead of the tube-plate. Also mesh screens protecting the ash-pan damper doors were fitted to add to the sprinkler system fitted in 1996. Just at this time the 'King' was on the threshold of an ambitious programme away from home territory, including visits to Crewe, Carlisle and York, and heavily-loaded rail-tours on the Settle & Carlisle line.

Working away from home, particularly in the north, turned out to be a patchy affair, mixing some lively performances with some which were less successful. The experiences highlighted what Swindon's designers knew instinctively and were truly expert at, that the traction they designed suited a particular length of railway and was the practical application of 'horses for courses'. In mitigation, problems with steaming on the S&C were largely caused by the defective seal to the smoke-box door which when remedied largely corrected the situation. Also not helping, it appeared that the new spark-arresting arrangements were resisting full and even draught across the full area of tubes — in effect reducing the flow of hot gases past the super-heater elements and the intensity of the draught on the fire — and needed modification.

The experiences in the north prompted some considerable food for thought. It was generally agreed that even without the smoke-box problems, the runs were over-loaded to the extent that the speeds attained were inadequate for optimum steam-generation. Another factor was the crewing, which, although in the skilled hands of the Crewe and Carlisle men, nevertheless lacked the necessary prior rehearsal on the locomotive. It was far from ideal that the first time many of the individual footplate men got their hands on No 6024 was when facing one of the country's premier main-line challenges, with 525 tons on the drawbar. The more practice they had, the better the running became.

The realistic conclusion is — and there is little doubt — that day in, day out, the 'Kings' on Western lines would never have been bettered by any other class and justified their '8P' classification, but conversely it couldn't be argued that hauling 12 or 13 coaches on the Long Drag or the WCML north of Preston, a 'King' would be the equal of a good Pacific. While it will take an exceptional performance by one of the preserved Pacifics to do

significantly better than No 6024 over the South Devon banks, it's highly unlikely that the 'King' will take any records over the S&C with such loads.

Latterly, *King Edward I* has been seen predominantly on home territory, and has returned to Plymouth unassisted on a number of occasions when it has demonstrated its ability to put almost all its power directly onto the rail without slipping. In August 2002 the 'King' broke the record for steam-haulage with the full permitted load, with the fastest ever start-to-stop time for the 52 miles from Plymouth to Exeter, in 58min 6sec.

In October 2002 with six months of its boiler ticket left, it was clear that the driving wheel tyres were too thin and the Society had no choice but to withdraw the locomotive. The decision was made to embark early on the second major overhaul, and this was duly carried out by the Society within the site of Tyseley Locomotive Works. Since its main-line reappearance in 1996, the engine had handled 66 rail-tours, running over 15,000 main-line miles. Thirty-three of these trains (50%) were formed of 13 Mark 1 coaches (about 520 tons).

Dick Blenkinsop

2004 to date

To keep pace with safety improvements the locomotive has been fitted with standard Train Protection Warning System (TPWS). The Society has also completed its water-carrier project for use on the main line enabling greater pathing flexibility and water-stops on Network Rail to be avoided on certain routes.

No 6024 returned to main-line activities in October 2004 again painted in British Railways livery and after running-in between Birmingham and Stratford-upon-Avon, undertook a busy main-line schedule based in the Midlands, the southeast and the southwest, completing 6,000 miles in its first 12 months back. In 2005, *King Edward I* achieved a major milestone in its history and on 2 July it celebrated its 75th Anniversary in great style, hauling a special train from Paddington to Kingswear. The previous Saturday, thanks to English, Welsh & Scottish Railways, it ran footplate rides inside Old Oak Common depot for over 100 Society Members and guests.

The locomotive then worked throughout the summer of 2005 on many trains in the southwest, and up to September completed almost 5,000 main-line miles before returning to the depot at Tyseley Locomotive Works for some well-earned maintenance time. 2006 has seen the prospect of another busy programme and yet more modifications in the form of the fitting of 'black-box' equipment, known as OTMR (on-train monitoring and recording).

Guest Appearances

The engine has made appearances at Open Days and other special events at Bescot, Gloucester, Exeter, Old Oak Common, Swansea and St Blazey. It has serviced and stabled at the depots at Old Oak Common, Stewarts Lane, Bounds Green, Aylesbury, Swansea Landore, Cardiff Canton, Newport Godfrey Road, Bristol's Bath Road, Barton Hill and St Philips Marsh, Gloucester, Worcester, Exeter Riverside, Plymouth Laira, St Blazey, Norwich, Peterborough and Carlisle Upperby.

It also appears in steam regularly at steam centres and on main-line-connected preserved lines. It has made visits to the former Great Western Works at Swindon, the Great Western Society at Didcot, the former Bulmers Railway Centre in Hereford, the Severn Valley Railway, Tyseley Locomotive Works, the West Somerset Railway, the Crewe Heritage Centre, the National Railway Museum in York, the Bodmin & Wenford Railway, the Paignton & Dartmouth Steam Railway, the Southall Steam Centre, the Yeovil Railway Centre, and the Watercress Line (Mid-Hants Railway).

The 6024 Preservation Society Limited

The Society was originally established to purchase the locomotive, restore it to main-line condition and maintain and operate it on the main line. An Exempt Charity, the Society is the owner of the locomotive and has been so for longer than the Great Western Railway and British Railways put together. The primary objective of the Society is to carry on maintaining the locomotive to the required standards in order that it is able to continue to work on Britain's railways.

4 October 2004 — Some of the Society's Working Party involved with the 2002-04 overhaul at Tyseley Locomotive Works. *Mike Wild*/Steam Railway

Opposite page: **31 August 2002** — Climbing to Dainton summit eastbound past Coombe Fishacre in the early evening on the record-breaking run between Par and Exeter. *Mark S. Wilkins*

The Society has almost 400 members, including life members. Each member is able to purchase shares in the Society which gives them a single vote. Having equal voting rights gives every member an equal stake in the 'King'. The Society is run by a Management Board which has the full range of the required skills to carry out the various duties and responsibilities; Board members are all volunteers, as are all the other active members. The core of the Society's funding is *Club 60-Twenty Four* which has almost 300 members who contribute in total nearly £3,000 every month. The *Club* offers a wide range of benefits to its members, such as main-line rail-tour tickets; events for members; opportunities for footplate rides on No 6024; and regular newsletters (in addition to three Society *King's Messenger* magazines in a year). With fees from main-line hire, work on private lines, donations and an associated company selling 6024 merchandise, the Society has been financially independent and self-sufficient. Full details of the Society's structure, its Membership options and activities can be found on the official website *www.6024.com* and the associated links to be found there.

The Day's Work

From dawn to dusk

Left: **18 March 2000** — On a fine early morning, waiting to depart from London Victoria to Minehead on the West Somerset Railway, via Swindon and Westbury. This was the first-ever visit by a 'King' to the London terminus. *Dave Fuszard*

Far left: **4 September 2005** — Sunrise at the EWS depot at Bristol Barton Hill, before the day's work on the 'Torbay Express' to Kingswear. *Kevin Blake*

Above: **20 February 1998** — Raising steam before a rail-tour in the early morning at the Great Western Society, Didcot. *Nigel Hunt*

Left: **25 February 1995** — Awaiting early-morning departure from Newton Abbot with the 'Royal Duchy' to Bristol and Swansea. *Colin Washbourne*

Right: **14 May 2005** — At the east end of Bristol Temple Meads on an early movement between the West Somerset Railway and Tyseley Locomotive Works. *John Chalcraft/Rail Photoprints*

Right: **7 December 1991** — Passing North Acton in the early morning on its way to Stratford-upon-Avon after the first Paddington departure for No 6024 for almost 30 years. *Brian Robbins*

Far right: **7 December 1991** — The same train now viewed from the River Cherwell in watery sunshine, storming past Kings Sutton on its way to Stratford-upon-Avon. *Ralph Ward*

Above: **10 January 1998** — Passing Tackley on its way to Birmingham Snow Hill and Worcester from Didcot with the 'Cathedrals Express'. *Brian Robbins*

Right: **14 March 1998** — On its first encounter with the S&C southbound from Carlisle, crossing the viaduct at Long Marton near Appleby. *Brian Bane*

Left: **9 June 2005** — With a high sun despite the early hour, running around the support coach at Battersea Sidings with the iconic Power Station in the background, before reversing into Victoria and starting the 'Cathedrals Express' to Bristol and return. *Huw Button*

Far left: **9 December 2000** — In early morning winter sunshine, passing Fenny Compton Junction northbound from Banbury to Birmingham International. *Mike Tyack*

Left: **6 October 2002** — Making a volcanic departure from its morning pick-up stop at Tyseley with the Birmingham Snow Hill to Paddington and return 'Inter City'.
Malcolm Ranieri

Right: **19 May 2001** — Passing Cogland Junction with a Paddington train from Minehead.
Andrew Bell

Below: **8 February 1990** — Running south in the early morning from Burton-on-Trent with the loaded Test Train from Derby to Banbury.
Phil Waterfield

Above: **30 January 1994** — Leaving Didcot on a fine early morning for Gloucester and Cardiff and return with the 'Red Dragon'. *Malcolm Ranieri*

Right: **8 February 1990** — Passing the flooded gravel pits at Lea Marston in the Tame Valley, on a sharp early morning, with the loaded Test Train from Derby to Banbury. *Ralph Ward*

Left: **11 December 2004** — With the exhaust hanging in the cold morning air, climbing through Bath on the outward leg of a Bristol-Paddington and return charter. *Pete Doel*

Right: **9 June 2005** — Observing a speed restriction at Twyford in a torrential downpour, with an outbound special to Bristol from Victoria and return. *Richard Lewis*

Below: **9 June 2005** — In better weather, pausing at Bath on its way to Bristol with a 'Cathedrals Express' from Victoria via Westbury. *John Chalcraft/Rail Photoprints*

Left: **9 May 1998** — An early departure from Bristol Temple Meads with the first 'King'-hauled passenger train into Cornwall, to Par. *Pete Skelton*

Right: **25 February 1995** — The 'Royal Duchy', now seen sprinting along the Teignmouth seawall, on its way to Bristol and Swansea. *Dick Blenkinsop*

Left: **1 March 1995** — Negotiating the points on the approach to Newport *en route* to Paddington from Swansea, before making its way to Didcot and northwards to BAD Kineton for its first overhaul.
Pete Skelton/Derek Short

Right: **4 June 2005** — Working hard as it approaches Ufton Nervet level crossing with a heavy 'Cathedrals Express' from London Victoria to Weymouth. *Geoff Plumb*

Left: **13 April 2002** — Passing Digbeth shortly after its morning start from Birmingham Snow Hill to run to Paddington and return. *Colin Washbourne*

Above: **28 December 1996** — Restarting the 'Bristolian' away from Didcot at Foxhall Junction in low winter light, after stopping for servicing, *en route* from Paddington to Bristol Temple Meads. *Geoff Plumb*

Left: **28 December 1996** — Passing Sydney Gardens, Bath with a 'Bristolian' from Paddington to Bristol Temple Meads and return. *Brian Bane*

Above: **26 March 1999** — Getting to grips with Shap's 1 in 75 in shocking weather on its way to Carlisle from Crewe. *Dick Blenkinsop*

Above: **16 April 1990** — Emerging from Wood End tunnel on the first revenue-earning trains over a weekend, between Tyseley and Stratford-upon-Avon. *John S. Whiteley*

Left: **1 March 1995** — Bursting out of the eastern portal of the Severn Tunnel with the 'Red Dragon' on its way to Paddington from Swansea. *Graham Morgan*

Right: **26 March 1999** — Now topping Shap summit surefootedly at little more than walking pace after an epic struggle in appalling weather. *John Cooper-Smith*

Above: **6 December 1997** — Sweeping around the curve at Shrivenham in low light with a Paddington-Bristol special. *Richard Lewis*

Right: **7 April 2002** — Following repairs after an attack of hot-boxes, running well at Henley in Arden on the first of two trains between Tyseley and Stratford-upon-Avon to prove that all was well. *Dave Richards*

Far right: **7 September 2005** — Passing Kings Sutton on the outbound leg of its marathon to Stratford-upon-Avon from Taunton, returning to Bristol. *Tim Easter*

Left: **1 March 1995** — Climbing from the Severn Tunnel towards Pilning with the 'Red Dragon' *en route* to Paddington from Swansea, with the new Severn Bridge under construction in the distance. *Pete Skelton*

Above: **24 April 1994** — Crossing the Thames at Maidenhead on its way to Stratford-upon-Avon from Paddington, the first steam-hauled passenger use of this section of the Great Western main line since No 6000 *King George V* left Paddington for Didcot as a part of the celebrations of that station's 125th Anniversary in 1979. *Graham Morgan*

Above: **2 October 1996** — Crossing Winterbourne viaduct after Bristol Parkway with the Hereford to Birmingham Snow Hill leg of the 25th anniversary celebration of the 'Return to Steam'. *Martyn Bane*

Left: **13 February 1999** — In steam at the Great Western Society, Didcot, beside a 1933 Super Saloon coach. *Dick Blenkinsop*

Right: **7 August 2005** — At Aller Junction with the returning 'Torbay Express' to Bristol Temple Meads from Kingswear. *Roger Siviter*

Right: **15 April 1990** — As first restored, running its first revenue-earning trains between Tyseley and Stratford-upon-Avon, at Henley-in-Arden. *Dick Blenkinsop*

Below right: **15 April 1990** — Newly restored, passing Bearley Junction on the first revenue-earning trains, between Tyseley and Stratford-upon-Avon. *Neville Wellings*

Far right: **31 March 2002** — Pausing at the London end of Birmingham Snow Hill station after arrival on the first train of the day from Worcester. *Dave Fuszard*

Left: **5 September 1999** — Into its stride approaching Parson's Tunnel, with a special from Paignton to Birmingham. *Bob Green*

Above: **9 May 1998** — Crossing Brunel's Royal Albert Bridge with the first 'King'-hauled passenger train into Cornwall, from Bristol to Par. The bridge, whose main piers are 455ft apart centre to centre, will be 150 years old in May 2009. *Cliff Woodhead*

Left: **28 February 2005** — Double-heading with No 7802 *Bradley Manor* through midday sunshine at Bishopsteignton beside the Teign estuary, on the VSOE 'Staite Pullman' from Taunton to Paignton and return. The train was run to celebrate the work of Bernard Staite. *Brian Robbins*

Above: **30 January 1994** — Leaving Hillfield Tunnel west of Newport and accelerating towards Cardiff, with the outbound leg of the 'Red Dragon' from Didcot. *Brian Robbins*

Left: **31 August 2002** — Approaching Dawlish westbound on the record-breaking run between Exeter and Par. *Andrew Bell*

Above: **31 August 2002** — A minute later passing Horse Cove. *Andrew Bell*

Above: **31 August 2002** — Approaching Dainton tunnel on the record-breaking run from Exeter to Par and return — well worth the £1 access fee to the field! *Richard Lewis*

Left: **8 September 2002** — Working a West Somerset Railway service train to Bishop's Lydeard, between Blue Anchor and Washford. *Mike Dodd*

Right: **9 May 1998** — Now well into Cornwall and making light of the task, crossing Forder viaduct on its way to Par, from Bristol. *David Holman*

Right: **30 November 1996** — A morning climb of Dainton bank double-headed with No 7325 from Plymouth to Worcester. *Mark S. Wilkins*

Far right: **9 November 1996** — Storming past Little Bedwyn in lovely sunshine, on the climb to Savernake with the Paddington-Plymouth 'Flying Dutchman'. *Paul Stratford*

Above: **6 May 1994** — Storming to the summit of Whiteball from Exeter, on its way to Bristol and Gloucester after the Rail Fair and its first visit to the Paignton & Dartmouth Steam Railway. *Graham Morgan*

Right: **28 December 1996** — Leaving Middle Hill tunnel with a Paddington to Bristol special, the second vehicle in a rather startling 'Disney' purple livery. *Don Bishop LRPS/Steam Recreations*

Above: **21 February 1998** — Restarting from Dorrington after watering, on its way from Newport to Shrewsbury, Chester and Crewe. *Mark Wilkins*

Left: **15 March 1997** — Setting off from Didcot and leaving a smokescreen across South Moreton with a charter to Minehead via the Berks & Hants. *Geoff Plumb*

Left: **18 March 2005** — On the West Somerset Railway, heading towards Minehead on the climb to Crowcombe, the first vehicle being a six-wheeled milk tank. *Don Bishop LRPS/Steam Recreations*

Above: **9 May 1998** — In perfect sunshine crossing St Germans viaduct with the first 'King'-hauled passenger train now deep into Cornwall on its way from Bristol to Par. *Bob Green*

Right: **27 July 2002** — Leaving Didcot eastbound for Reading before taking the Berks & Hants to Taunton and Minehead, with an HST slowing down, as a gesture of respect perhaps? *John Whitehouse*

Far right: **19 May 2001** — Bathed in brilliant midday sunshine, climbing eastbound from Middle Hill Tunnel towards Box tunnel on a special from Minehead, double-headed from Bristol with No 5029 *Nunney Castle* to Swindon and London. *Mike Tyack*

Right: **1 March 1995** — 140 miles into its journey from Swansea, accelerating the 'Red Dragon' towards London past the site of the water-troughs at Goring. *Malcolm Ranieri*

Below: **9 November 1996** — Storming past Crofton on a bright morning on the climb to Savernake with the Paddington to Plymouth 'Flying Dutchman'. *Bob Green*

Far right: **28 February 2005** — Hauling the VSOE Pullman stock with No 7802 *Bradley Manor* alongside the Teign estuary on the outbound 'Staite Pullman' between Taunton and Paignton. *Huw Button*

Above: **10 January 1998** — Crossing the mirror-like River Avon at Eckington on its way from Worcester to Kemble and Didcot. *Bob Green*

Right: **25 February 1995** — Approaching the entrance to Parson's tunnel along the seawall near Teignmouth with the 'Royal Duchy', just avoiding cloud obscuring the early morning sunshine. *Mike Dodd*

Right: **9 October 1994** — Climbing towards Churston at Waterside on a Paignton & Dartmouth Steam Railway service to Kingswear. *Colin Washbourne*

Below right: **18 June 2005** — The whiter than white exhaust indicates a bad incidence of priming on a fine hot day at White Waltham after the Maidenhead stop on the 'Cathedrals Express' from Victoria to Gloucester and return. *Tim Easter*

Far right: **9 May 1998** — Crossing Coldrennick viaduct with the first 'King'-hauled passenger train into Cornwall, with just 20 miles to go to its destination at Par. *Mike Goodfield*

Above: **25 February 1995** — Sweeping inland at Langstone Rock on its way to Exeter and beyond with the 'Royal Duchy'. *Mike Tyack*

Left: **28 February 2005** — Pausing at Torquay on the 'Staite Pullman' from Taunton to Paignton, double-heading with No 7802 *Bradley Manor* hauling the VSOE Pullman stock. *Nathan Williamson*

Right: **19 September 1998** — Rounding the curve by Langstone Rock on its way to Penzance from Exeter, the first 'King' ever to run to the end of the West of England main line. *Mike Goodfield*

Above: **15 April 1990** — Making a fine sight when newly-restored, at Spring Road, on a Tyseley-Stratford-upon-Avon special. *John Cooper-Smith*

Left: **7 April 2002** — Working well on a fine day at Wood End on a running-in turn between Stratford-upon-Avon and Birmingham. *Bob Green*

Right: **25 February 1995** — Storming up Whiteball bank from Exeter with the 'Royal Duchy' to Bristol and Swansea. *Graham Morgan*

Right: **26 October 2002** — On a clear autumn day, sweeping around Horse Cove, on a Birmingham-Kingswear and return charter. *Bob Green*

Far right: **9 June 2005** — On a fine morning, climbing past Crofton Pump House on the outbound leg to Bristol via Westbury from Victoria. The House was originally built to accommodate the canal pumps. *Pete Doel*

Above left: **22 March 2000** — A Minehead service train passing Nethercott on the West Somerset Railway. *David Holman*

Left: **19 September 1998** — Entering Cornwall over Brunel's Royal Albert Bridge on its way to Penzance from Exeter, the first 'King' ever to run to the end of the West of England main line. *Richard Jones*

Above: **25 February 1995** — Hammering to Whiteball summit on the 'Royal Duchy' from Newton Abbot to Bristol and Swansea. *Andrew Bell*

Right: **7 August 2005** — The westbound 'Torbay Express' rounds the curve to Teignmouth station on its way to Kingswear from Bristol.
Don Bishop LRPS/Steam Recreations

Above: **26 October 2002** — Going well past Shaldon Bridge beyond Teignmouth in fine sunshine, on a Birmingham to Kingswear and return charter. *Neville Wellings*

Left: **4 June 2005** — In fine summer light, climbing to Savernake alongside the Kennet & Avon canal, on a heavy Victoria-Weymouth special. *Pete Doel*

Far left: **18 December 2005** — Accelerating hard at West Wycombe in low winter sunshine on the climb to Saunderton on a Paddington special to Stratford-upon-Avon and return. *Bob Green*

Above: **19 September 1998** — Crossing Moorswater viaduct, west of Liskeard on an Exeter-Penzance rail-tour, well towards the end of the West of England main line.
Neville Wellings

Right: **25 February 1995** — Climbing over Whiteball summit with maximum effort on the 'Royal Duchy' and approaching the tunnel, on its way to Bristol and Swansea.
Mike Goodfield

Above: **18 June 2005** — Climbing Sapperton bank at Thrupp on a blazing afternoon, on the return 'Cathedrals Express' between Victoria and Gloucester. *Rave Richards*

Right: **20 September 1998** — In lovely autumn sunshine, crossing Collegewood viaduct at Penryn on the Falmouth branch, returning to Bristol and on to Swindon. *Mike Tyack*

Left: **26 March 1999** — Racing towards Penrith between Wreay and Southwaite in early spring evening light on the southbound climb to Shap summit, soon after departure from Carlisle for Preston and Crewe. *John Cooper-Smith*

Above: **14 August 2005** — Servicing at Paignton on the Paignton & Dartmouth Steam Railway, to prepare for the return to Bristol after the outbound 'Torbay Express' has turned at Churston. *Matthew Carey*

Above: **20 September 1998** — Crossing Coldrennick viaduct near Menheniot, on the return from Falmouth to Bristol Temple Meads. *Brian Bane*

Right: **7 August 2005** — Approaching Kennaway tunnel west of Dawlish on the down 'Torbay Express' (viewed from the last coach). *Huw Button*

Far right: **31 July 2005** — Reversing past Waterside on the Paignton & Dartmouth Steam Railway before the return 'Torbay Express' from Kingswear to Bristol. *Nathan Williamson*

Right: **25 February 1995** — Bursting out of Whiteball Tunnel with the 'Royal Duchy' from Newton Abbot to Swansea and starting its rapid descent of Wellington bank.
Martyn Bane

Far right: **14 March 1998** — Blasting across Birkett Common, on its first encounter with the S&C southbound from Carlisle.
John Cooper-Smith

Above: **6 October 1994** — Arriving at Kingswear with a Paignton & Dartmouth Steam Railway service train. *Mike Spencer*

Right: **25 February 1995** — Now carrying a different head-code, continuing this epic run climbing Filton bank Bristol at Narroways Hill Junction before heading into Wales through the Severn Tunnel and on to Swansea. *Brian Bane*

Above: **25 February 1995** — Climbing Filton bank at Horfield, Bristol, before going into Wales through the Severn Tunnel and on to Swansea. *Dick Blenkinsop*

Right: **9 May 1998** — With just a few miles to go, crossing Largin viaduct with the first 'King'-hauled passenger train into Cornwall, from Bristol to Par. *Pete Doel*

Right: **14 March 1998** — On its first encounter with the S&C from Carlisle, fighting across Mallerstang Common after a slack, still with a couple of miles to go to the summit at Ais Gill. *John Whitehouse*

Far right: **2 July 2005** — Climbing the upper reaches of Wellington bank to Whiteball Tunnel in gloomy light, with the westbound leg of the 'Anniversary Limited', a special charter, which ran from London Paddington to Kingswear, to celebrate the locomotive's 75th birthday. *Dave Richards*

Left: **28 March 1998** — toiling across Ribblehead viaduct on the troubled second northbound run on the S&C.
Martyn Bane

Far Left: **31 March 2002** — Erupting from Rainbow tunnel, Worcester, on the afternoon train returning to Birmingham Snow Hill.
Neville Wellings

Left: **22 March 1992** — Pausing for water at Banbury on the returning 'William Shakespeare Express' to Paddington from Stratford-upon-Avon. *Dick Blenkinsop*

Below: **9 November 1996** — In late afternoon, roaring past the site of Wellington station, with the Paddington-Plymouth 'Flying Dutchman'. *Mark S. Wilkins*

Right: **7 September 2005** — Hurrying past Bishops Itchington in the late afternoon on the return leg of its marathon Taunton-Stratford-upon-Avon and return to Bristol. *Ralph Ward*

Above: **2 July 2005** — Powering past Cockwood Harbour near Starcross on the inbound leg of the 'Anniversary Limited', a special charter to celebrate the locomotive's 75th birthday. The train ran from London Paddington to Kingswear and returned to Taunton. *Matthew Carey*

Left: **26 February 2005** — Storming up the Lickey Incline in a nasty drizzle and failing light, on the return to Birmingham after a special to Newport. *John Whitehouse*

Right: **7 August 2005** — Racing through the evening light past Dawlish with the return 'Torbay Express' from Kingswear to Bristol. *Don Bishop LRPS/Steam Recreations*

Left: **7 August 2005** — On a clear, fine summer evening at Burlescombe, climbing towards Whiteball summit with the return 'Torbay Express' from Kingswear to Bristol. *Mike Tyack*

Above: **26 October 2004** — Climbing Campden bank at Mickleton on a Society promotion from Worcester to London. *Bob Green*

Left: **22 March 1992** — Accelerating away from Bearley Junction in the evening on the returning 'William Shakespeare Express' to Paddington from Stratford-upon-Avon. *Paul Stratford*

Below: **22 March 1992** — Crossing Souldern viaduct at sunset on the returning 'William Shakespeare Express' to Paddington, from Stratford-upon-Avon. *Malcolm Ranieri*

Right: **31 July 2005** — An evening rest at Newton Abbot with the 'Torbay Express' after a brake problem at Ware Barton. *Nathan Williamson*

Left: **14 August 2005** — Evening arrival in Platform 5 at Taunton working the return 'Torbay Express' from Kingswear. *Brian Garrett*

Below: **7 August 2005** — Crossing the Huntspill on the Somerset levels, close to sunset, on the 'Torbay Express' returning to Bristol from Kingswear. *John Chalcraft/Rail Photoprints*

Right: **7 August 2005** — The same location looking west at the returning 'Torbay Express'. *Pete Doel*

Above: **31 August 2002** — Sweeping through the evening light beside the Teign estuary at Bishopsteignton, on the return leg from Par to Exeter. *Pete Doel*

Right: **26 October 2002** — Resting at Taunton on a Birmingham-Kingswear and return charter. *Brian Garrett*

Above: **2 February 1992** — Taking water at Banbury after nightfall before proceeding to Paddington from Stratford-upon-Avon. *Mike Spencer*

Right: **2 February 1992** — Passing Anyho Junction on the night-time return from Stratford-upon-Avon. *Dave Smith*

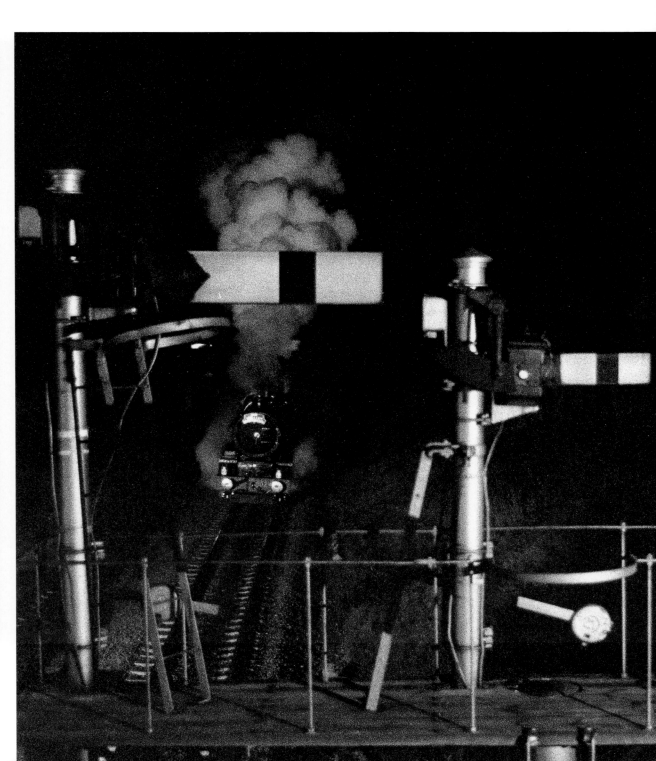

Above: **2 February 1992** — Arriving in Paddington's No 1 platform, from Stratford-upon-Avon. *Mike Spencer*

Right: **26 October 1991** — Posing in steam under floodlights at the annual photo evening held be the Great Western Society at Didcot. *Richard Lewis*

Left: **6 December 1997** — Preparing for the restart of the 'Bristolian' from Bristol Temple Meads to return to Paddington. *Dick Blenkinsop*

Above: **21 October 2004** — Pausing at Stratford-upon-Avon on the third loaded test train from Tyseley, which ended in a week of successful main-line trials. *Mike Wild*/Steam

Left: **6 December 1997** — Preparing for the restart at Bristol Temple Meads of the 'Bristolian' to Paddington. *Dick Blenkinsop*

Right: **17 April 1994** – Pausing for water at Kemble in the dark after the climb of Sapperton bank on a train positioning the locomotive from Kidderminster to Didcot. *Mike Spencer*

Right: **11 October 1997** – Arrival back in Paddington's Platform No 1 after returning from Bristol. *Dick Blenkinsop*

Far right: **9 November 1996** – Passing Totnes at nightfall and starting the climb of Rattery bank with the Paddington-Plymouth 'Flying Dutchman', double-headed with Mogul No 7325. *Mike Spencer*

Above: **6 October 2002** — On a clear night, awaiting the road at Leamington before powerfully tackling Hatton bank, on its return to Birmingham Snow Hill from Paddington. *Graham Morgan*

Right: **24 November 1990** — With an ETHEL behind the tender for train heating, night arrival at Banbury from Derby before returning to Didcot. *Dick Blenkinsop*

Above: **1 March 1995** — After an earlier arrival from Swansea, the 'Red Dragon' awaits its departure from Paddington to Didcot. *Martyn Bane*

Right: **25 October 1996** — The end of the day's work, at the Great Western Society, Didcot. *Mike Tyack*

Diary of Events

1990

When the locomotive returned to traffic, steam-hauled passenger trains were restricted to a handful of secondary main-line routes, often without entering busy centres. Light engine movements were possible on certain principal routes, but at night. The 'King' was further barred from some routes because of its height. Therefore, ambitions were limited to getting onto the main-line and trusting that the work would materialise, rather than having any high hopes of retracing the steps of the 'Kings' in their heyday.

8 February 1990

Derby to Tyseley via Banbury; 122 miles; Test train 11 coaches; Fine, cold, turning to drizzle

This was the locomotive's first appearance on the main line since June 1962. After an uneventful light-engine and coach run north from Tyseley to Derby two days earlier, followed by a day spent weighing and balancing the locomotive at the Derby Technology Centre, a storming effort was put on to Banbury, with nothing held back. This revealed a minor irritant in the form of melted white metal on the outside cross-head slippers, but this didn't prevent a trouble-free return to Tyseley, with the engine progressing all the way tender-first! Most observers agreed that no 'King' had climbed Hatton Bank tender-first on the same day it had been to Derby! A 'first'! Despite the crosshead problem, this was an impressive first outing, promising an exciting future.

20 March 1990

Tyseley to Burton on Trent and return; 62 miles; Test train Engine + support coach; Damp, cold

The repeat test run to Derby ended at Burton in disappointment, with a recurrence of the problems.

5 April 1990

Tyseley to Stratford-upon-Avon and return; 77 miles; Test train Engine + support coach; Fine

Third time lucky, and at last everything stayed cold and solid after it had been discovered that the cause of the problems had been the outside slide-bars being 'pinched' by their safety straps. Thankfully this run was uneventful and was a big step forward.

15/16 April 1990

Tyseley to Stratford-upon-Avon and return x eight; 320 miles; 13 coaches; Sunny, snow flurries, rain

This was the first revenue-earning work for 28 years. In harness with the Birmingham Railway Museum's 'Castle' class No 5080 *Defiant*, four return trains on each day were run between Stratford and Birmingham. The two locomotives alternated in each direction and while the 'King' handled the heavy load of mixed stock with its expected muscle, the 'Castle' also performed magnificently. Everyone went home happy after an exhausting weekend, enjoying some high quality work, setting new standards for GW 4-6-0s — and No 5080 was a revelation!

17 May 1990

Tyseley to Didcot; 73 miles; Engine only; Fine

In early May the engine went to Bescot. This was another first, the first of many visits to an MPD Open Day. Then a light-engine cruise to the Great Western Society at Didcot to get into position for a prestige event in a couple of days .....

19 May 1990

Didcot to Stratford-upon-Avon and return; 167 miles; nine coaches; Fine

The annual InterCity staff outing, know as the 'VIP Special', with the 'raspberry ripple' Mark 1 stock, returning as far as Banbury, then light-engine back to the Great Western Society. The locomotive's reputation for putting on exciting displays was enhanced, the light load allowing good, high speed work.

24 June 1990

Newport to Shrewsbury and return; 188 miles; 12 coaches; Overcast

An overnight movement to Bulmers at Hereford preceded a light-engine run down to Newport before the first genuine long-haul run, on the 'North and West'. Many understandable questions comparing the locomotive with No 6000 *King George V* were emphatically answered and, despite the regular speed restrictions due to over-bridge clearances north of Newport, the locomotive handled the heavy train of Pullmans in great style. Of particular note were the impressive ascents of the severe banks to Llanvihangel and Church Stretton in both directions, punctuated by some free-running high speeds including 83mph at Dorrington. This was followed by an overnight light-engine movement to Swindon, where the former GWR Works was hosting the *NRM on Tour* exhibition. And where does the locomotive stable? Next to *KGV*, in Shop No 19!

30 June/1 July 1990

Swindon to Gloucester and return; 73 miles; Engine + support coach; Fine

This was to attend another Open Day, this time at Gloucester, with shuttles along a short stretch of line by the Yard. The engine won lots of goodwill, before returning to Swindon for more showing-off, and to celebrate the loco's 60th birthday alongside No 6000. A fortnight later the engine made the short run back to Didcot. The GWS was becoming home, with plenty of GW engines there, as well as the newly-restored BR Pacific No 71000 *Duke of Gloucester*.

24 November 1990

Didcot to Derby and return; 253 miles; 12 coaches (+ ETHEL); Overcast
The second-ever visit of a 'King' to Derby, with a mighty load of over 500 tons. The outward leg was handled efficiently, with a high power-output ascent of Hatton bank in excess of 1,900edbhp, and swift work north of Birmingham. The return was less impressive, a badly-clinkered fire inhibiting free-steaming, so the climb from Leamington to Fosse Road was taken at a crawl. Work with the fire-irons at Banbury helped and with no major adverse gradients ahead the delays were not too great. A lesson learned was the need to clean the smokebox at the service point. The poor steaming on the return was attributed to unburned coal accumulating in the smokebox, gradually hampering the draughting. Skip-loads of char were removed from the smokebox at the end.

So the first year back on the main line ended. After an uncertain start the locomotive and those looking after it quickly gained confidence and with almost 1,700 main-line miles on the clock the loco was increasingly earning a place in people's minds as a star performer. It was impossible to predict what the next year would bring, but the encouraging aspect was that the 'understudy' of No 6000 King George V was being offered mainline work. Early in 1990 there had been no certainty of this.

1991

12 January 1991

Didcot to Derby and return; 253 miles; 12 coaches (+ ETHEL); Fine, frosty
Derby again! Another massive load, but this time the inbound leg was as good as the outbound. The frozen air made for wonderful exhaust effects, captured for posterity on PSOV footage, with another powerful ascent of Hatton. The return was exhilarating, particularly the climb to Fosse Road

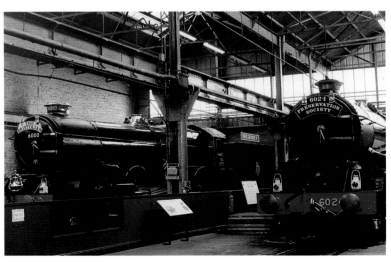

from Leamington and will be remembered for the cheeky run through Oxford by Archie Davis, the Didcot driver, who consequently got into deep hot water, especially as we had left the relief guard behind at Saltley! This was a mechanically trouble-free run and full of easily-generated effort, partially due to restarting from Derby with a clean smokebox.

17 March 1991

Didcot to Derby and return; 253 miles; 12 coaches; Fine
Again! This was with a slightly easier load without the ETHEL, but made even more entertaining for the passengers by the involvement of ex-S&DJR '7F' 2-8-0 No 53809 around the Sheffield circular. Passengers enjoyed another high quality performance by the locomotive, which was well on top of the job, in the hands of enthusiastic and skilled footplatemen. This time the approach to Oxford was almost sedate, but by the time the station had been passed speed had increased by 30mph! More hot water for Archie! Overall, most agreed this was another good, consistent performance by No 6024.

Above: **2 July 1990** — On its 60th birthday, positioned on the traverser to move into Swindon Works No 19 Shop. *Colin Washbourne*

Left: **2 July 1990** — The only time since 1962 that No 6000 and No 6024 met up, in Swindon Works No 19 Shop, on No 6024's 60th birthday. *6024 Archives*

2 February 1992 — Climbing towards High Wycombe over Denham viaduct in an early morning thick fog on a Paddington to Stratford-upon-Avon and return special. *Dave Smith*

6 May 1991

Didcot to Stratford-upon-Avon and return; 135 miles; 10 coaches; Fine
This was No 6024's share of a pair of shuttles in the day. The 'King' went out in the morning and back in the evening, while BR Pacific No 71000 *Duke of Gloucester* did its return legs during the day. It was an interesting day for the enthusiasts, with two highly contrasting locomotives each giving the passengers a great time! The return was taken at a good pace with startling acceleration down Hatton bank after rejoining the main line, but delayed at Banbury by another absentee guard! Following this run, a routine examination revealed that the LH radius rod of the Walschaerts valve-gear had suffered damage, resulting in the stripping down of the inside motion and the repair of the rod.

15/18 August 1991

Didcot to Old Oak Common; 101 miles; five locomotives + support coaches; Fine
Leading No 71000 *Duke of Gloucester*, No 5029 *Nunney Castle*, No 3440 *City of Truro* and No 6998 *Burton Agnes Hall*, the locomotive set out for London for its first visit to the capital for almost 30 years, but disgraced itself by suffering the failure of both injectors at Reading. With all that spare power the convoy eventually made it safely to Old Oak, where a three-day event was held, attended by many thousands of people. As there was time enough to repair the injectors, an uneventful return was made to the Great Western Society.

9 September 1991

Swindon to Hereford; 148 miles; 12 coaches; Fine
Running light and towing the Society's newly-acquired (but unpainted) Mark 1 support coach, the loco ran to Swindon to attach to this charter. It then made its first revenue-earning passage of the Golden Valley. After a lengthy drought throughout the region the vegetation was tinder-dry, and between them, the 'King' and GWR 4-4-0 No 3440 *City of Truro* (which left Lydney running north during the morning) caused a number of line-side fires. The operations authorities accordingly arranged for a Class 37 to pilot the train on from Newport, although there was little doubt which locomotive was working the harder on the ascent of Llanvihangel bank!

21 September 1991

Chester to Hereford; 94 miles; 12 coaches; Fine
An early morning light engine movement from Bulmers — where the locomotive had shared stabling facilities with ex-LMS '8F' No 48773 from the Severn Valley Railway — to Chester preceded an exciting run back to Hereford in glorious sunshine, and included a powerful climb of Gresford bank. The '8F' returned the train to Chester, while the 'King' stabled at Bulmers for a couple of weeks.

7 October 1991

Hereford to Swindon; 148 miles; 10 coaches; Drizzle, damp
Allowing for the fact that this was the first loaded climb of the steep side of Sapperton bank, the train weight was restricted but in the event the locomotive made the task look easy. The engine and coach returned to Didcot light. This was a competent run, which went uneventfully.

7 December 1991

Paddington to Stratford Upon Avon and return; 238 miles; 10 coaches; Frosty
For many, this was **the** run. Back in Paddington for the first time in preservation and running along the 'New Road' via High Wycombe, the run attracted considerable interest. Unfortunately, the event was overshadowed by a very bad accident in the Severn Tunnel the same morning, involving a number of fatalities. The light engine and coach movement from Didcot had taken place early that morning. The locomotive slipped a great deal on the frosty rails on the adverse gradients through the Chilterns, but a good performance from Princes Risborough on the singled section kept the schedule under control. All round, this was a very successful outing, with some classic 'King' noises on a classic route and the sight of the locomotive in Paddington was a treat for everyone.

So ended the locomotive's second year back, during which it completed 1,600 miles. The engine was gaining a growing reputation for being able to handle whatever it was asked to do and this was taking it further afield although not yet commanding greater quantities of work. Other reasons for satisfaction were its solid mechanical reliability and it was also benefiting from the skills of the different footplate crews who were now getting on the engine, including the elite link of enginemen from Marylebone depot who had made such a name for themselves in the 1980s. It was also becoming obvious that hints were being dropped of a number of new routes being made available and cautious optimism for the future of steam was becoming infectious.

1992

2 February 1992

Paddington to Stratford-upon-Avon and return; 238 miles; 10 coaches; Cold, damp, heavy mist

The second 'William Shakespeare Express' started badly with a delay due to dragging brakes on the stock. Engineering work added to the problems resulting in only steady progress to Gerrards Cross. An energetic climb of Saunderton salvaged some pride and the loco reached 77mph before Bicester but overall the run was disappointing with many checks.

22 March 1992 *(Table 1)*

Paddington to Stratford Upon Avon and return; 238 miles; 11 coaches; Fine

This run was beset with a number of difficulties, with at the end, easily the worst imaginable. After a late start from Paddington another guard was found AWOL, so 45min was lost at Gerrards Cross while he caught up! A viaduct collapse at Leamington Spa required 'wrong-line working' in the down direction which further delayed matters. On the return, due to a signal fault, the train was directed towards Marylebone at South Ruislip and had to set back, losing hard-fought for punctuality by causing a delay of almost 30min. Finally, the approach to Paddington was made on the Up Main (rather than the Up Relief on which there was an engineering possession for resignalling works at Royal Oak) and it was discovered in the worst possible way that the locomotive was out of gauge. Travelling at about 20mph under the skew girder-bridge carrying Ladbroke Grove, a stud of the safety-valves just caught the underside of the steel bridge and there had to be only one loser.

A huge explosion was followed by a roar of steam sounding not unlike a jet engine on full throttle. The valves and brass bonnet were propelled at high velocity into the metalwork of the bridge, with most of the debris rebounding into the back of the tender; the train was deluged with water. The forward momentum of the locomotive was just sufficient to avoid the debris hitting the cab so it was a miracle that none of the footplate crew was injured. Despite the shock they instantly experienced, the crew of Ernie Stewart (Traction Inspector), Gordon Read (Driver) and Bob Cotterill (Fireman) had the presence of mind to shut the fire-hole door, apply the brakes and try to fill the boiler, but the sudden loss of steam reduced pressure so quickly that the injectors could not work properly.

In the meantime, the explosion had been heard around the neighbourhood, and, mindful of IRA activity then current, the emergency services were immediately called. Within two minutes the Fire Brigade was on the scene. Bob Cotterill by this time was attempting to 'drop' the fire, but to avoid any risk the Brigade hosed the fire and put it out. Control closed Paddington to all traffic in and out. The track was searched for debris and eventually a Class 47 pilot locomotive was hooked on and the train dragged into Paddington's Platform No 1, two hours late. Unfortunately, this incident caused many delays and cancellations of a number of service trains. The PA at Paddington explained the problems by announcing that

Table 1: 22 March 1992

LONDON PADDINGTON to STRATFORD Upon AVON and return

Load: 11 coaches - 401 tons tare, 425 tons gross
Crew: *Driver* R Whittington (to Banbury), V Waite (to Stratford), G Read (to London)
Fireman E Feasey (to Banbury), A Davies (to Stratford), R Cotterill (to London)
Traction Inspector A Bryant (to Banbury), J Slater (back to Banbury), E Stewart (to London)
Weather: Fine, sunny, dark on return after Banbury

Distance Miles		Schedule	Actual	Speeds
	PADDINGTON	0	0.00	start
3.31	Old Oak Common W. Jn.	9	9.22	26
7.54	Greenford W Jn.	15	16.11	18
10.19	South Ruislip	21	21.52	21
14.73	Denham	--	27.35	65
17.33	GERRARDS CROSS	44	30.39	stop
9.14	High Wycombe	22	13.13	26
14.11	Saunderton	--	20.55	46
17.40	PRINCES RISBOROUGH	35	27.02	stop
5.88	Haddenham	--	6.17	68
12.62	*Brill and Ludgershall*	--	12.29	69
15.49	*Blackthorn*	--	14.52	67
18.58	Bicester N.	24	18.06	51
24.41	*Ardley Tunnel*	--	26.27	52
27.61	*Aynho Jn.*	37	35.02	28
29.15	Kings Sutton	--	37.58	44
32.66	BANBURY	47	44.57	stop
3.71	*Cropredy*	--	8.13	45
6.11	*Claydon Crossing*	--	11.13	49
8.75	Fenny Compton	12	14.06	60
14.41	*Harbury Tunnel*	--	26.51	49
19.98	Leamington Spa	26	38.44	5
21.83	WARWICK	30	43.20	stop
4.15	Hatton	6	10.22	15
9.63	*Bearley W Jn.*	18	18.42	36
13.39	STRATFORD Upon AVON	25	24.45	stop
0.00	STRATFORD Upon AVON	0	0.00	start
2.65	Wilmcote	--	7.27	25
3.76	*Bearley W Jn.*	7	9.36	34
9.24	Hatton	19	19.02	15
13.39	WARWICK	25	26.33	stop
1.85	LEAMINGTON SPA	8	4.57	stop
7.01	*Greaves Siding*	--	14.26	stop
11.20	Fenny Compton	13	23.10	44
16.26	*Cropredy*	--	30.13	52
19.98	BANBURY	33	40.43	stop
3.51	Kings Sutton	--	10.38	40
5.05	*Aynho Jn.*	10	13.52	19
8.25	*Ardley Tunnel*	--	19.40	45
14.08	Bicester N.	20	30.15	20
23.42	*Ashendon Jn.*	--	41.11	75
26.78	Haddenham	--	43.58	64
32.66	PRINCES RISBOROUGH	43	54.19	stop
3.29	Saunderton	--	7.00	58
5.13	*MP 19/II*	--	8.42	70
8.38	High Wycombe	15	13.19	24
17.40	GERRARDS CROSS	30	25.39	stop
2.60	Denham	--	4.06	64
5.30	West Ruislip	--	6.18	77
7.14	South Ruislip	13	11.47	stop
14.02	Old Oak Common W. Jn.	25	66.04	20
15.98	*Ladbroke Gr. (overbridge)*	--	70.55	stop
17.33	PADDINGTON	37	152.30	stop

BANBURY to LONDON EALING BROADWAY				
Load:	11 coaches - 401 tons tare, 425 tons gross			
Crew:	*Driver* B Axtell			
	Fireman R Cotterill			
	Traction Inspector A Bryant			
Weather:	Fine, sunny, hot			
Distance		**Schedule**	**Actual**	**Speeds**
Miles	BANBURY	0	0.00	*start*
5.05	*Aynho Jn.*	--	--	*stop*
8.25	*Ardley Tunnel*	--	--	49
14.08	Bicester N.	26	27.00	30
20.04	*Blackthorn*	--	--	78/80
23.42	*Ashendon Jn.*	--	--	71
26.78	Haddenham	--	--	74
30.01	*Ilmer*	--	--	67
32.66	PRINCES RISBOROUGH	49	43.00	*stop*
3.29	Saunderton	--	--	43
5.87	*West Wycombe*	--	--	62
8.38	High Wycombe	--	--	40
17.40	GERRARDS CROSS	30	27.00	*stop*
2.60	Denham	--	--	66
5.30	West Ruislip	--	--	75
12.34	West Ealing	--	--	sigs
13.08	EALING BROADWAY	58	65	stop

'an old steam engine has broken down'. The next day the London *Evening Standard* headlined the event with 'Vintage train runs out of puff'.

No 6024 was towed to Old Oak Common. The following day was spent closely examining the still-hot boiler and firebox for any discernible damage resulting from the massive thermal shock. Replacement safety-valves and a brass bonnet were located and within 16 days the locomotive was ready for a steam test.

To mark their heroic roles on that evening, Ernie, Gordon and Bob were presented with framed photographs of the locomotive by the Society, as was the local Fire Brigade.

4 May 1992

Swindon to Newport via Gloucester and return; 162 miles; 10 coaches; Fine
After a light engine return to Didcot in late April which proved that the disaster at Ladbroke Grove had had no ill effects, the engine made its way to Swindon for the first of its runs for the *Bristol Evening Post*. The line through the Golden Valley and along the Severn estuary was becoming a regular route for the engine, and a strong eastbound climb of Sapperton was the highlight of the day, demonstrating that the locomotive had, by some distance, plenty in hand still on this tricky climb.

12 July 1992 (Table 2)

Ealing Broadway to Stratford-upon-Avon and return; 238 miles; 11 coaches; Fine
This run was particularly notable for the very fine handling by Driver Brian Axtel — who, having never stepped on the locomotive before (and never again either!), took to it like a 'natural' — and his mate Bob Cotterill on the return. Together, through sheer skill, they shifted the loco-

motive's work up a gear and from being merely exciting, it became magnificent! Those who were there will never forget that exhilarating dash through the evening glow between Aynho Junction and High Wycombe (including 80mph at Blackthorn) and a sprint through the suburbs, to make up time lost after getting the wrong road at Aynho. Arrival in London was only seven minutes down.

30/31 August 1992

Aylesbury to Quainton Road and return x 16; 221 miles; 5 coaches; Fine
The engine made its much-awaited return by rail to Quainton Road, its home for 16 years and the site of its restoration. Top-and-tailing No 6024 with 'Castle' class 4-6-0 No 5029 *Nunney Castle*, these unique steam-hauled shuttles out of Aylesbury over the whole weekend drew plenty of visitors to the Quainton Railway Centre. This was another first for the 'King', representing its class for the first time on this part of the network. Following the return to Didcot, melted white metal was detected around the right-hand outside big-end which was removed, re-metalled and replaced.

12 November 1992

Didcot to Tyseley; 73 miles; 13 coaches; fine, mild, mostly in darkness
This was the return of an outbound charter to the Great Western Society by the Great Central Railway and positioned the 'King' for work in the Midlands. A gentle run allowed the new bearing to settle down.

6/13 December 1992

Tyseley to Stratford-upon-Avon and return x eight; 360 miles; 10 coaches; cold, damp
Stabled at Tyseley with a number of locomotives, including LMS Pacific No 46203 *Princess Margaret Rose* and LNER 'A3' Pacific No 4472 *Flying Scotsman*, the 'King' then returned to this familiar route on successive weekends paired with the 'Princess' for the popular Christmas shuttles and ended 1992 in Birmingham.

In 1992, the Society, for the first time since the locomotive's return to the main line, saw some of the more difficult challenges facing steam locomotive owners operating on the modern railway. Although on balance the year ended positively, with more mileage than ever, first the bridge incident and then later the mechanical problem focused attention on just how difficult this 'hobby' was becoming. However, the work was increasingly flowing in and the supporting volunteers were coping well.

1993

9 January 1993

Tyseley to Didcot; 73 miles ; 9 coaches; cold, fine
This positioning move returned the 'King' to Didcot, but without the support coach which remained at the BR depot at Tyseley for bogie repairs and wheel-turning.

21 March 1993

Ealing Broadway to Stratford-upon-Avon and return; 238 miles; 11/12 coaches; fine
Another 'Shakespeare' from London along the High Wycombe line with some lively work on the climbs and sustained high speed from the restart at Princes Risborough to passing Bicester. The 6024 support coach was delivered to Stratford by a Class 47 and hooked onto the engine for the return to London. The climb up the 1 in 75 from Stratford to Wilmcote was sure-footed. Shortage of coal forced a conservative run beyond Banbury.

12 April 1993

Gloucester to Newport and Hereford and return; 174 miles; 11 coaches; Fine
This was another good run along the Severn estuary and the engine coped well with the arduous work on the 'North & West' between Newport and Hereford. The engine turned on the triangle within the Bulmers factory for the final time (Bulmers subsequently withdrew from all its previous involvement with steam locomotives and removed the track of one of the chords of the triangle to release land for development of its factory).

22 August 1993

Didcot to Worcester and return via Oxford and Gloucester; 157 miles; 12 coaches; fine
This run contained a number of 'firsts': the first run ever by No 6024 along the Cotswold Line and the Midland route from Worcester to Gloucester (probably by any 'King'); a load of 12 coaches up the steep eastbound climb of Sapperton which it handled with ease; and the first steam-hauled passenger train along the Great Western main line between Swindon and Didcot for many years.

1993 was a light year in terms of the mileage accumulated (just over 1,000 miles) and disappointing from this angle. But in other ways it was very significant. The changes within the railway industry preparing for privatisation were strongly suggesting many new steam routes were becoming available, although there were still strongholds of resistance remaining in some zones; for instance, soon the full 77 miles between London and Swindon would accommodate steam-hauled passenger trains, but perversely getting beyond Swindon to Bristol was still out of the question. These signs predicted a rapid increase in routes and 1994, the final full year before the expiry of No 6024's first boiler ticket, was to see opportunities never dreamed of in 1990.

1994

30 January 1994

Didcot to Cardiff via Gloucester and Newport and return; 235 miles; 12 coaches; fine
The Society took a gamble and promoted its first main-line charter, the 'Red Dragon'. Capitalising on the availability of new routes, the itinerary

again included the 24-mile section of the Great Western main line between Didcot and Swindon and the additional 12 miles to Cardiff from Newport. Seeing the welcome by the steam-starved people of Cardiff on arrival was worth the ticket price on its own! A full train added to the significance of the event but a Class 47 was added to the formation for train-heating for some of the outbound and all of the return; the resulting load of over 600 tons on the drawbar was risky and unsurprisingly the climb of Sapperton eastbound was tortured and nerve-wracking, culminating in a massive wheel-slip which erupted at the tunnel entrance, at which point the diesel took its own weight. A great day overall but that load on Sapperton was not an experience to be repeated.

4 April 1994

Bristol TM to Newport via Gloucester and return; 163 miles; 12 coaches; fine
On 18 March the locomotive travelled from Didcot to London for an Open Day at Old Oak Common and then to the Severn Valley Railway for a period. From there the engine and coach ran to Bristol Temple Meads to run this rail-tour, again sponsored by the *Bristol Evening Post*. Significantly, this was the first scheduled steam-hauled passenger train in

19 March 1994 — Steaming outside the 'Factory' at Old Oak Common on an Open Day. *Colin Washbourne*

141

Brunel's great station since the GWR 150 Celebrations in 1985. Bristol and its surroundings had been barred to steam ever since, due to local management objections (although a few weeks previously an engineering possession had earlier forced the authorities to allow Bulleid Light Pacific *Taw Valley* to make an unscheduled diversion and stop there). The route included the climb of Filton bank to Bristol Parkway and Westerleigh Junction and then through Cheltenham to Gloucester. Yet more new routes were opening up.

17 April 1994

Kidderminster to Didcot via Cheltenham and Swindon; 119 miles; 12 coaches; fine

This run returned the locomotive from the Severn Valley Railway to the Great Western Society. It involved a tender-first movement to Stourbridge Junction and an ECS move back to Kidderminster before returning to Didcot over what was becoming a very familiar route. The engine again coped competently with the load on Sapperton eastbound.

24 April 1994

Paddington to Stratford-upon-Avon and return to Didcot; 190 miles; 12 coaches; fine

4 September 1994 — Disguised as No 6026 *King John,* passing Charfield between Gloucester and Bristol. *Graham Morgan*

Following a light engine move to London, this was the first use of the Great Western main line from Paddington through Reading with a passenger train in preservation since *KGV* made its ill-fated one-way run to Didcot in 1979 as a part of the Paddington 125 celebrations. Throughout the day the engine put on an exciting performance in the hands of the Acton and Didcot crews who appeared to be enjoying themselves!

29 April 1994

Gloucester to Exeter via Bristol TM; 113 miles; 12 coaches; fine

For many months the Exeter Railfair at the Riverside depot had been planned and the Society was invited to exhibit No 6024. Positioning trains were arranged and after a light move to Gloucester from Didcot the engine made the first steam-hauled passenger train movement to Exeter since 1985. Unquestionably 'the star of the show', the 'King' was in light steam for the four day event and drew many onlookers. The then-owner of *Flying Scotsman* stepped onto No 6024's footplate briefly, offering to swap the A3 for the 'King', but was politely turned down! After the event, the engine headed westwards light with the support coach along the South Devon sea-wall to the Paignton & Dartmouth Steam Railway, where it ran service trains for a couple of days. Another first!

6 May 1994

Exeter to Gloucester via Bristol TM; 113 miles; 12 coaches; fine

The return movement from Exeter was another exciting run with plenty of energy on the climb to Whiteball and an exhilarating race across the Somerset levels. The locomotive stabled at Gloucester until a night-time light engine movement back to Didcot, in readiness for its next outing in an increasingly hectic programme.

20 May 1994

Gloucester to Swansea via Chepstow and Newport; 102 miles; 12 coaches; dull, drizzle

Although in BR days No 6024 ended up shedded at Cardiff it never got west of there in traffic so this was another first for the engine. A two-day visit to Swansea, including being parked in the station for the benefit of visitors, was a good way for people to see the 'King' and the engine drew a lot of interest. The run westwards attracted huge line-side crowds; the engine's running was uneventful and it handled its load well on this demanding route.

22 May 1994

Swansea to Didcot via Newport, Chepstow and Gloucester; 162 miles; 12 coaches; cloudy, turning fine

The return was marred by poor footplate work from the outset. First the Swansea fireman was so taken with the attention the engine was receiving that he forgot to shovel much coal on the fire. This brought about an automatic brake application on the down-slope from Stormy Sidings short of Bridgend, through lack of steam! At this point the driver concluded that the vacuum system was at fault. After the necessary blow-up the train was restarted and made steady but very late progress towards Newport but with very heavy water consumption due to the constant use of the large ejector. At Cardiff an enforced stop to take water was necessary and it eventually transpired that at the stop on the open line the driver had opened the vacuum valve on his side of the cab, causing a constant leak of vacuum. The train eventually arrived at its destination with some very glum faces.

4 September 1994

Didcot to Bristol TM via Kemble and Gloucester and return; 194 miles; 12 coaches; fine
The opportunity was offered to run with different name and number plates, so after the necessary modifications to cab-sides and buffer-beam, the engine was disguised as No 6026 *King John*. Regrettably, the running was mediocre throughout the day despite the boiler pressure appearing to be permanently fixed at 250psi for about 12 hours. It was no surprise to discover afterwards that the consumption of water (18,000gal) and coal (12 tons) were ludicrously excessive. If a 'King' had demonstrated this economy in Great Western days say between London and Exeter (*via* Bristol, 193 miles), the fireman would have been sacked and if a regular event the entire class would have been withdrawn by 1932!

2 October 1994

Newport to Paignton via Severn Tunnel and Bristol TM; 130 miles; 12 coaches; fine
In late September the locomotive moved light from Didcot to the Severn Valley Railway for a couple of weeks and then to Newport to position for this train. This was the first steam-hauled passenger train through the Severn Tunnel for many years and the first time for No 6024 since 1962. The engine then proceeded onto the P&DSR for a couple of weeks.

16 October 1994

Newton Abbot to Didcot, via Bristol TM and Badminton; 130 miles 12 coaches; dry, overcast
This was a journey of fits and starts and endless water-stops, punctuated by some loud work from the 'King'. The locomotive worked superbly between Exeter and Tiverton with a maximum of 68mph at MP178 but was robbed of a fine speed at the summit of Whiteball by the AWS leaking on. There was also some excellent work from Taunton to Worle Junction where service traffic from the Weston branch then slowed proceedings. After Bristol the running was more subdued with a maximum of 72mph at Little Somerford.

26 November 1994

Didcot to Worcester via Bristol TM; 131 miles; 12 coaches; fine, mild
This was another positioning movement to get the locomotive from Didcot to the Severn Valley Railway over the Christmas period. This was

26 November 1994 — Kenneth Leech, aged 102, stands on the footplate for the first time in over 30 years, during a station stop at Chippenham. *Dick Blenkinsop*

the locomotive's first passage of this section of the Great Western main line since 1962 and included 82mph down Dauntsey bank. As the train was booked to stop at Chippenham, the Society invited the 102-year-old Kenneth Leech to visit the engine while it stood in the station. This was the great man's first visit to Chippenham station since the end of steam! Sadly, in December 1994 Kenneth suffered a fall in the street and died in January 1995.

This had been the locomotive's busiest year yet. Almost 2,700 main-line miles were completed with some fascinating visits to different locations, as well as regular running on familiar routes. Satisfyingly, the engine thank-

NEWTON ABBOT to SWANSEA via BRISTOL TEMPLE MEADS

Load: 12 coaches (+ Class 47 to Exeter) - 442 tons tare, 470 tons gross
Crew: *Drivers* B Hayton (to Exeter), N Hellawell (to Bristol)
Firemen R Cox (to Exeter), R Westlake (to Bristol)
Traction Inspectors G Petrie (to Exeter), J Jons (to Bristol)
Weather: Fine, sunny, dry

Distance		Schedule	Actual	Speeds
Miles	NEWTON ABBOT	0	0.00	*start*
5.19	Teignmouth	--	9.10	54
9.64	Dawlish Warren	11	15.08	51.5
15.06	*Exminster*	--	20.34	65
19.24	Exeter St. Thomas	--	24.33	*sigs*
20.16	EXETER St. DAVIDS	23	28.26	*stop*
1.20	*Cowley Bridge Jn.*	3	3.45	
3.56	*Stoke Canon*	--	6.55	52
8.31	*Hele and Bradninch*	--	12.16	56
12.41	*Collompton*	--	16.47	56
14.62	Tiverton Jn.	19	19.09	48.5
19.72	*Whiteball Summit*	--	25.52	35
	Whiteball tunnel (East)	--	27.01	47
23.53	*Wellington*	--	29.29	83
26.17	*Bradford Crossing*	--	31.18	84
	MP 167	--	31.5	83.5
30.60	TAUNTON	35	35.51	*stop*
4.60	*Cogload Jn.*	6	6.40	65
11.45	Bridgwater	13	12.29	70
17.57	Highbridge	--	18.02	67
25.08	*Uphill Jn.*	29	24.31	68
28.01	*Worle Jn.*	32	27.02	68.5
32.64	Yatton	--	31.10	70
36.59	Nailsea and Backwell	--	34.31	66
38.54	*Flax Bourton*	--	36.23	62
42.67	Parson Street	41	40.34	45
44.59	BRISTOL TEMPLE MEADS	54	48.28	*stop*
0.00	BRISTOL TEMPLE MEADS	0	0.00	*start*
1.60	Stapleton Road	--	6.03	39
4.78	Filton	10	12.16	30
5.94	Patchway	--	14.09	36
8.73	*Cattybrook*	--	17.34	69 *sigs*
9.51	Pilning	16	20.43	25
10.99	*Severn Tunnel East*	--	22.48	60
15.34	*Severn Tunnel West*	--	26.42	54
16.46	Severn Tunnel Jn.	24	28.00	50
22.45	*Llanwern*	--	35.08	57
26.33	NEWPORT	41	42.56	*stop*
9.13	Rumney River Bridge Jn.	--	18.12	40
11.75	Cardiff General	20	23.28	21
22.88	Pontyclun	33	38.51	40
25.75	*Llanharan summit*	--	43.18	29
31.88	Bridgend	44	51.09	25 *check*
33.38	MP 192	--	54.27	46
35.88	*Stormy Siding*	--	57.30	52
37.38	Pyle	--	58.58	72
38.38	*MP 197*	--	59.44	82
39.88	*MP 198/II*	--	60.47	88
40.13	*Margam Moors Jn.*	--	60.58	86
44.11	Port Talbot	57	64.19	60
47.80	Briton Ferry	--	68.31	40
49.63	Neath	64	73.01	15 *check*
51.70	Skewen	--	77.45	32
57.46	SWANSEA	76	91.04	*stop*

---

fully had been almost mechanically perfect throughout the year and was putting in more strong performances which repeatedly attracted a solid core of loyal enthusiasts. Significantly, however, the engine's height was never far away from people's thoughts; it was, for instance possible to take a passenger train down to Paington but because of an over-bridge at Torre any up return had to be taken 'wrong-line', so the only permitted movement was light-engine and support coach only.

1995

1 January 1995
Kidderminster to Didcot via Kemble; 119 miles; 12 coaches; fine, cold
This train moved the locomotive back to Didcot before a period of runs prior to the end of the boiler ticket. The usual strong climb of Sapperton indicated an engine in fine fettle rather than one ready for a full overhaul!

5 February 1995
Paddington to Paignton via Bristol TM; 222 miles; 12 coaches; fog, cold, wet
This was the first leg of a triangular plan, first taking the engine to the P&DSR for a couple of weeks. Initially carrying the 'Cornish Riviera' headboard to depart from Paddington, this was then switched for passing Chippenham, when a 'Kenneth Leech Memorial' headboard was proudly carried. This headboard was presented to members of Kenneth's family who travelled on the train. The run was again very energetic with a loud and smoky climb of Wellington bank in appalling conditions.

25 February 1995 *(Table 3)*
Newton Abbot to Swansea via Bristol TM; 180 miles; 12 coaches; cold, frosty at first, then fine
This was a rail-tour which had everything. It was run on classic Great Western routes including the long climb to Whiteball and the sprint down Wellington, followed by Brunel's flat track to Bristol, the climb to Filton, then the Severn Tunnel, and finally the tough road to Swansea and all day the engine was pushed very hard. No 60009 *Union of South Africa*'s run down Wellington the previous week might have had something to do with it. On Whiteball the edge was taken off things rather by some over-enthusiastic firing but even so a creditable speed of 84mph was reached at Wellington. Some hurried smokebox cleaning in Temple Meads revived an ailing fire and there then followed one of the fastest runs by steam to Swansea ever known. The high-speed entry into the Severn Tunnel and then spending only 3min 54sec in the tunnel with an approximate 80mph at the bottom gave a clue as to what was to come and working to a 76min HST schedule for the section between Newport and Swansea the locomotive made complete mincemeat of the road, culminating in an estimated drawbar horse-power output of over 1,900 on the climb to Stormy sidings and a maximum of 88mph down the bank. But for a number of checks the run would have been even quicker. With about two-and-a-half shovels of coal left in the tender arrival in Swansea was 16min late, but somehow nobody seemed to care! This perfor-

5 February 1995 — Pounding up Wellington bank to Whiteball tunnel in shocking conditions, with nothing spared. *Eddie Sturgeon*

mance was put into perspective when compared with the 121min schedule allowed for the midweek 'Red Dragon' in steam days.

1 March 1995

Swansea to Paddington and Didcot via Badminton; 249 miles; 12 coaches; cloudy then fine

The last long-distance rail-tour before the locomotive disappeared to its 'secret' location for a full overhaul was a great way to go out but inevitably it was also tinged with just a hint of dejection. Following a late departure from Swansea, as usual, the locomotive put on an adequate show with some lively running between Newport and the Tunnel and was given mile after mile of the Up Main of the Great Western main line after Didcot, but the running was pedestrian due to numerous signal checks. No-one really wanted this to be the final run and for everyone the end of the boiler ticket had arrived far too soon. This mood seemed to dominate everyone present; others, perhaps also sensing the end of an era as BR entered its twilight, saw a special occasion in the offing. Almost every BR employee from west of the Severn wanted to travel to London in the support coach that day.

The time had passed so quickly. The locomotive's performance had remained top class for almost the entire length of the ticket and a full over-haul seemed premature. Arrangements had been made for an overhaul site with a main-line-connected, fully equipped private facility, rather than go to Quainton Road or negotiate space on a preserved line. Accordingly, after arriving at Didcot, the engine watered and then tiptoed away into the night, to the military base at BAD Kineton near Fenny Compton.

After only 18 months hard work, a much-modified 'King' saw daylight again and on a fine 23 September 1996 with the support coach moved from BAD Kineton to Kidderminster, passing through the new Birmingham Snow Hill station. The overhaul completion had been planned around the end of the summer of 1996, in order for No 6024 to be ready to haul a series of trains retracing the steps of pioneer classmate No 6000 King George V. These rail-tours were arranged to celebrate the 25th Anniversary of the 'Return to Steam' in 1971. A running-in turn with coaches had been planned for 23 September but a fire-ban imposed by Railtrack reduced the operation to a gentle amble in the new air-brake mode to the Severn Valley Railway for 10 days gentle running.

1996

2 October 1996

Hereford to Birmingham SH via Severn Tunnel and Didcot; 12 coaches; 176 miles; fine

After no running-in miles at all at speed, No 6024 made a light engine move from Kidderminster to Hereford via Malvern for the first celebra-

running between Solihull and Hatton including 81mph at Lapworth and, despite some intermittent periods when steam was short, put in a solid effort on the undulating route to London. At the arrival at Paddington it was apparent that the water consumption had been high. After servicing and turning, the train proceeded powerfully to Didcot without any dramas, but unusual sounds from the chimney were getting picked up, indication of a steam 'blow' past pistons or valves.

9 November 1996

Paddington to Plymouth via Westbury; 13 coaches (with No 7325 from Newton Abbot); 226 miles; fine

A month was spent at Didcot investigating the unusual sounds which had been observed and, surprisingly, rectifying a couple of broken piston-rings and loose piston heads. The engine had to be fully fit, because the next scheduled run was the much-anticipated return to Plymouth, No 6024's base for many years in Great Western days. In charge of 510 tons, the work by No 6024 over the Berks & Hants route was good throughout (another return for the engine after over 30 years) and included 80mph at Castle Cary, but a late restart from Exeter and watering problems at Newton Abbot marred an otherwise punctual run. This caused the section to Plymouth to be run in the dark, but few can have failed to enjoy the syncopated sound of the rapid exhaust beat of the pilot engine and the slower, heavier beat of the 'King', alternately working harmoniously and in discord, evocative of the memorable days of heavy double-headed trains over the route. Both engines performed impeccably on the climbs and laid the foundation for many successful steam rail-tours over the route during the next decade.

30 November 1996

Plymouth to Kidderminster via Bristol TM and Worcester; 13 coaches (with No 7325 throughout); 193 miles; fine

This rail-tour returned both locomotives to the Severn Valley Railway. The section to Exeter was performed without any bother, but throughout the day it was increasingly obvious that the 'King' was not steaming well. At the time it was felt that working the train unassisted from Exeter would have suited the locomotive better because double-heading required less effort and therefore the firebox didn't maintain optimum heat. Arrival at Kidderminster was with the 'Mogul' increasingly doing the work, testament to the extraordinary endurance and power of this little locomotive. In the meantime, the conditions in the firebox of the 'King' continued to deteriorate and it ended the day with an almost dead bed of solid clinker on the grate. The 'King' stabled at Bridgnorth but only got there courtesy of the 'Mogul'.

27 December 1996

Worcester to Didcot via Kemble; 12 coaches; 89 miles; damp, cold

This was an uneventful positioning movement back to Didcot from the Severn Valley Railway in readiness for a major railtour the following day.

9 November 1996 — In full cry climbing at Hungerford Common on a fine morning as it makes its way west on the 'Flying Dutchman' from London Paddington to Plymouth.
Geoff Plumb

tion train. Considering all the renewed motion (including new pistons) was very tight and the locomotive was not unduly pressed, it did a good job, particularly on the climbs before Maindee and after the restart from Bristol Parkway the work up to Chipping Sodbury and the run down the other side was competent. Running to a generous schedule to Banbury the locomotive kept good time but after a late restart due to other traffic a much tougher schedule was beyond No 6024 and despite a good climb of Hatton bank Birmingham was reached 31min late. This was the first time No 6024 had entered Snow Hill station with a passenger train since the early 1960s. In Snow Hill short speeches were made by the key people who had been involved in Bulmers' initiative with *KGV* 25 years before to the very day; then the engine unhooked and made its way to Tyseley.

5 October 1996

Stourbridge Junction to Paddington via Birmingham SH and High Wycombe, return to Didcot; 12 coaches; 176 miles; fine

The next leg of the 25th Anniversary run started at Stourbridge Junction (with a diesel banker) because the train was too long for the platform length at Snow Hill. The engine was still very stiff but achieved some fast

28 December 1996

Paddington to Bristol TM; 13 coaches; 118 miles; cold, fine

An uneventful outbound run saw a decent performance although the big load and a series of checks prevented anything sensational. During the servicing layover in the depot, a leak developed in a new armoured brake-pipe between the engine and tender, resulting in the loss of the air-braking. Repairs could not be completed in time and the train was returned to Paddington diesel-hauled while the engine returned to Didcot under its own steam in vacuum-brake mode with the support coach.

So, despite the promise of new and interesting times on the railway and after all the hard work put in by everyone on the overhaul, 1996 ended disappointingly. The brake-pipe problem was a set-back but modifications were carried out and this particular hitch didn't recur. More worrying was the inconsistent performance of the locomotive, with unreliable steaming and high water consumption. Immediately into 1997 after the return to Didcot, the pistons were stripped down again and yet again, broken piston-rings and loose piston heads were discovered. The conclusion reached was that the new piston-heads were marginally over-sized for the cylinder bores. Moreover, the outside cylinder bores had been scored. The solution was for the outside cylinders to be fitted with liners and the piston heads to be machined down to suit, but with slightly increased clearance. Unfortunately this caused the locomotive to miss a couple of rail-tours, but the time was well worth spending to sort out the problem.

1997

15 March 1997

Didcot to Taunton and the West Somerset Railway, via Reading and Westbury; 13 coaches; 123 miles; fine, becoming cloudy and wet

Taken gently at first to ensure the repaired pistons and cylinders were behaving, it gradually became evident that the engine was transformed, once again running freely and steaming easily and economically. Speed was gradually built up to Reading and then the engine was given its head, making strong and rapid climbs to Savernake and Brewham accompanied by healthy sounds from the chimney and taking the downhill sections freely and efficiently. With a sense of relief all round, the engine arrived at, for it, a brand new location and was given a rousing welcome on the West Somerset Railway. The train ran through to Minehead with GW 'Castle' class No 7029 *Clun Castle* as pilot engine.

5 April 1997 *(Table 4)*

Taunton to Plymouth and return; eight coaches; 161 miles; fine

This run signalled that the barriers truly were coming down. The previous November, the reprofiled 'King' had succeeded in the ambition to steam to Plymouth. Now, it was going there again, *unassisted!* True, the authorities had insisted that it should only be loaded with eight coaches but nevertheless the success of this rail-tour was *the* break-through which

TAUNTON to PLYMOUTH and return

Load: 8 coaches - 288 tons tare, 323 tons gross
Crew: *Driver* B Dudley-Ward
Fireman G Ewans
Traction Inspector not recorded
Weather: Fine, sunny, dry

Distance		Schedule	Actual	Speeds
Miles/Ch.	TAUNTON	0	0	start
1.22	*Silk Mill LC*	--	--	28
10.68	*Whiteball tunnel (East)*	--	17	--
11.38	*Whiteball Summit*	--	--	50
15.78	Tiverton Jn.	24	23	--
22.29	*Hele and Bradninch*	--	--	74
30.60	Exeter St Davids	41	37	35
35.47	*Exminster*	--	--	73
41.22	Dawlish Warren	53	47	69
50.74	NEWTON ABBOT	67	60	stop
1.09	*MP 215 (Aller Jn.)*	--	--	29
3.73	*Dainton tunnel (East)*	--	--	31
8.67	Totnes	17	16	stop
13.27	*MP 227/II Rattery*	--	--	33
17.76	*MP 232 Wrangaton*	--	--	46
21.05	*Ivybridge*	36	37	47
25.04	*Hemerdon*	43	44	51
29.69	PLYMOUTH NORTH ROAD	51	52	stop
0.00	PLYMOUTH NORTH ROAD	0	0	start
4.00	*Plympton*	--	--	49
6.65	*Hemerdon*	18	--	24
10.56	*Ivybridge*	24	17	56
13.76	*MP 232 Wrangaton*	--	--	54
23.09	Totnes	40	30	59
25.76	*MP 220*	--	--	61
27.76	*MP 218*	--	--	46
28.00	*Dainton Tunnel W (in)*	--	--	41
30.67	*MP 215 (Aller Jn.)*	--	38	stop
31.76	Newton Abbot	53	43	pass
37.04	Teignmouth	--	49	sigs
45.16	*Exminster*	--	--	67
52.03	EXETER St. DAVIDS	75	71	stop
1.20	*Cowley Bridge Jn.*	5	3	27
8.31	*Hele and Bradninch*	--	--	60
14.65	Tiverton Jn.	--	21	54
19.72	*MP 174 Whiteball Summit*	--	--	48
23.52	*Wellington*	--	--	76
30.61	TAUNTON	42	38	stop

would open up all sorts of opportunities on this route both for the 'King' and many other locomotives.

With a revitalised, free-running engine due to its regular use since its arrival at the West Somerset, a light load, a tender full of Welsh steam coal, an enthusiastic crew in the shape of the *maestro* Bryan Dudley-Ward and his right-hand man Geoff Ewans and, to cap it all, fine weather over a classic 'King' route, unsurprisingly the train was a sell-out. There were no disappointments on this day. A sedate climb of Wellington bank gave no hint of what was to come and once Geoff had adapted his technique to the slow-burning character of the coal, the performance thereafter was nothing short of sensational. Despite standing starts from Newton Abbot (water) and Totnes (signals) the westbound climbs of

SWANSEA to DIDCOT

Load:	13 coaches - 478 tons tare, 506 tons gross
Crew:	*Drivers* C Parry (Bristol Pky), B Dudley-Ward (to Didcot)
	Firemen G Ewans (to Bristol Pky.), C Parry/G Ewans (to Didcot)
	Traction Inspector G Jones
Weather:	Overcast, continuous rain

Distance		Schedule	Actual	Speeds
Miles/Ch.	SWANSEA	0	0.00	*start*
7.67	Neath	19	17.54	30
9.53	Briton Ferry	--	20.40	47
13.28	Port Talbot	28	24.45	53
17.23	*Margam Moors Jn.*	--	29.10	54
21.22	*Stormy Siding*	--	34.58	31
25.42	Bridgend	46	40.39	56
34.47	Pontyclun	60	52.03	57
39.07	*MP 177*	--	56.27	61
45.57	Cardiff General	76	66.04	*pass*
57.40	NEWPORT	96	85.35	*stop*
3.61	*Llanwern*	--	6.40	55
9.66	Severn Tunnel Jn.	16	12.45	55
10.76	*Severn Tunnel West*	17	14.01	52
15.25	*Severn Tunnel East*	--	18.19	67
16.62	Pilning	24	20.17	40
18.49	*Patchway tunnel W*	--	23.10	34
19.49	*Patchway tunnel E*	--	25.22	23
21.50	BRISTOL PARKWAY	37	33.49	*stop*
4.50	*Westerleigh Jn.*	11	7.47	46
8.14	*Chipping Sodbury tunnel W*	--	11.59	54
17.46	*Hullavington*	27	21.18	73
28.67	WOOTTON BASSETT UGL	41	33.28	*stop*
5.52	Swindon	12	12.12	50
16.36	*Uffington*	25	22.06	72
18.75	*MP 64 (Challow)*	27	24.09	75
29.44	DIDCOT West UGL	40	44.07 *sigs*	*stop*

Dainton and Rattery showed just what the engine was really made for. If anything, the climbing of Hemerdon and Dainton on the return was even better, with a full 13min gain on the schedule by Aller Junction. There were many beaming faces on the platform at Taunton after the on-time arrival that evening.

17 May 1997
Paignton to Gloucester via Bristol TM; 13 coaches; 148 miles; fine at first, then heavy rain, dark after Bristol
The locomotive remained at the WSR for about a month before running this rail-tour which moved it to the SVR. This first involved a tender-first light engine and POB run to Paignton before departing for Gloucester. Fine, punctual work to Bristol was dramatically halted by a tropical-style rainstorm while the loco watered in Temple Meads, which caused the flooding of a culvert on Horfield bank. After a considerable delay the train proceeded to Gloucester. Despite the delay the locomotive performed impeccably with reliable steaming and losing no time, a clear indication that the improvements resulting from the repairs were being sustained.

27 September 1997
Gloucester to Hereford via Worcester and Ledbury; 12 coaches; 58 miles; fine
Scheduled to take a train from Gloucester to Carmarthen and back, this run was cut short by another air-brake fault, this time the failure of the compressor. Shortly after the water-stop at Ledbury the pump failed and the train had to proceed slowly to Hereford where it was terminated. The engine and support coach returned in vacuum mode to the SVR. On test the pump worked perfectly and a temporary lubrication problem was diagnosed.

11 October 1997 *(Table 5)*
Swansea to Paddington; 13 coaches; 193 miles; overcast, continuous rain
This rail-tour involved almost 200 miles of light engine movement, first to get the engine to Swansea, and then to take it to Didcot from London. On this tough, undulating route, run in filthy weather, the load was inevitably going to be a factor, but despite this and a late start the locomotive was on top of the job all day. To emerge from the Severn Tunnel at 47mph with over 500 tons was some effort. The best running was to Didcot, seeing some good speed after Swindon and but for signal checks before arrival at Didcot which wasted over nine minutes arrival would have been early; thereafter a series of more signal checks enforced a frustratingly subdued run to Paddington but even so arrival in Platform No 1 was only a couple of minutes down. Overall, this was a fine performance on a route which captures many typical features of western lines and the locomotive was near to being back to its best.

6 December 1997
Paddington to Bristol TM and return; 13 coaches; 237 miles; cold, fine
Poor steaming bedevilled the outbound run beyond Didcot, resulting in the unusual decision to throw out the fire at Bristol. A temporary brake niggle delayed the start of the return but the running was much brighter with some lively work after Swindon including a pleasant cruise up to Paddington.

1997 ended much better than it started with the engine properly fit again for the first time since March 1995. However, with all the contributing factors, including the banning of all steam between the beginning of June and the end of August to avoid lineside fires, the amount of work done by the engine was below average, with 1,400 main-line miles completed. 1998 dawned with a large and ambitious programme planned, including a month of intensive work in the North of England with two runs in each direction on the Settle & Carlisle and a further first being a run to York and a visit to the National Railway Museum.

1998

10 January 1998 *(Table 6)*
Didcot circular, via Birmingham SH, Worcester and Kemble; 11 coaches; 200 miles; cold, sunshine, darkness after Gloucester

DIDCOT to GLOUCESTER via BANBURY and return via KEMBLE

Load:	11 coaches - 410 tons tare, 430 tons gross
Crew:	*Drivers* A Roseblade (to Worcester), R Churchill (to Didcot)
	Firemen A Llewelyn (to Worcster), F Sutton (to Didcot)
	Traction Inspectors G Jones (to Worcester), K Treeby (to Didcot)
Weather:	Dry, fine, sunny

Distance		Schedule	Actual	Speeds
Miles/Ch.	DIDCOT	0	0.00	start
5.25	Radley	--	14.27	52
10.31	Oxford	21	20.11	43
13.22	Wolvercote Jn.	26	23.39	56
22.11	Heyford	36	32.15	70
27.72	Aynho Jn.	43	37.28	69
29.45	Kings Sutton	--	38.54	70
33.06	BANBURY	49	44.28	stop
4.04	Cropredy	--	8.14	49
8.6	Fenny Compton	9	13.41	61
14.36	Harbury Tunnel (north)	--	19.32	53
19.71	Leamington Spa	22	26.01	28
21.64	Warwick	--	28.41	49
25.78	Hatton	31	33.51	41
30.15	Lapworth	--	39.17	47
32.59	DORRIDGE	40	46.25	stop
3.3	Solihull	--	7.03	54
10.41	Birmingham Snow Hill	18	19.20	30
17.41	Old Hill tunnel (east)	--	35.34	38
18.02	Old Hill tunnel (west)	--	36.15	46
22.42	Stourbridge Jn.	46	44.55	30
26.04	Blakedown	--	55.04	sigs
29.12	Kidderminster	58	60.07	57
44.16	WORCESTER SHRUB HILL	85	84.12	stop
0.00	WORCESTER SHRUB HILL	0	0.00	start
14.65	Ashchurch	24	22.53	68
21.76	Cheltenham Spa	33	29.51	43
28.36	GLOUCESTER	45	42.15	stop
7.17	Standish Jn.	14	13.41	27
11.72	Stroud	22	20.08	35
14.61	Brimscombe	--	24.09	51
18.11	Sapperton Tunnel (north)	--	29.23	27
19.15	Sapperton Tunnel (south)	--	31.33	30
23.06	KEMBLE	48	37.29	stop
4.05	Minety	--	7.08	59
13.56	SWINDON	22	22.57	stop
10.64	Uffington	16	14.35	35 check
13.23	MP 64 (Challow)	--	17.52	52
23.72	DIDCOT West End	32	31.15	stop

Table 6: 10 January 1998

CREWE to CARLISLE

Load:	13 coaches - 480 tons tare, 515 tons gross
Crew:	*Drivers* R Hatton (to Blackburn), G Hodgson (to Carlisle)
	Firemen R Hart (to Blackburn), P Kane (to Carlisle)
	Traction Inspectors K Treeby (to Blackburn), J McCabe (to Carlisle)
Weather:	Blustery wind, showers

Distance		Schedule	Actual	Speeds
Miles/Ch.	CREWE	0	0.00	start
8.80	Winsford Jn.	10	13.17	34
16.50	Weaver Jn.	--	24.07	59
24.15	Warrington	29	31.15	67
27.50	Winwick Jn.	--	33.45	66
35.90	Wigan	41	42.33	62
48.25	Farrington Jn.	59	56.00	26
49.20	Lostock Hall Jn.	73	60.59	pass
58.25	BLACKBURN GL	93	78.54	stop
0.60	Daisyfield Jn.	4	3.45	pass
5.15	Langho	--	--	check
10.80	Clitheroe	24	34.51	38
24.40	Hellifield	49	55.40	pass
27.65	Settle Jn.	52	60.19	60
29.65	Settle	--	62.46	45
35.70	Horton in Ribblesdale	--	72.41	33
40.40	Ribblehead	--	82.57	29 check
42.45	Blea Moor tunnel (south)	74	87.53	23
46.55	Dent	--	94.32	31
49.80	GARSDALE	86	100.20	stop
9.95	Kirkby Stephen	17	14.25	61
20.60	APPLEBY	34	26.10	17
11.05	Langwathby	17	16.16	50
20.85	Armathwaite	33	26.25	59
30.85	CARLISLE	52	37.30	stop

21 February 1998

Newport to Crewe via Shrewsbury and Chester; 11 coaches + Class 47(heating); 158 miles; fine

During the previous months the Society had been busy fabricating spark-arresting screens for the smokebox and the ash-pan damper doors. The screens were duly fitted for this run (which was planned to position the engine for its series of runs on the S&C), and the final section between Chester and Crewe — by which time it would be dark — was arranged for a visual trial of the new screens. The trial was a success, in that the sparks thrown from the chimney were of a small size and they extinguished while still airborne. However, the latter half of the run featured deteriorating steaming and by the time the train arrived at Crewe the engine had a very dull fire. This run positioned the engine for the first time in Crewe, in readiness for its much-awaited sparring with the S&C.

7 March 1998 *(Table 7)*

Crewe to Carlisle via Blackburn and Hellifield; 13 coaches; 157 miles; dull, wet, windy

Considering the load, this was a good performance overall, featuring some lively running on the WCML. The engine's first visit to the northbound face of the S&C, in foul weather, was unspectacular but competent and

Overall this was a very successful and punctual run and, despite a temporary brake problem on four coaches between Banbury and Dorridge, the engine made an energetic climb of Hatton before a violent slip. Another good climb of Sapperton in the dark was the highlight, the bright running back from Swindon being hampered by a long permanent way restriction at Uffington.

15 April 1998 — Opposite *Lode Star*, from which it is directly descended, standing on the turntable in the National Railway Museum's Great Hall. *Dick Blenkinsop*

BRISTOL TEMPLE MEADS to PAR				
Load:	9 coaches - 325 tons tare, 355 tons gross			
Crew:	*Driver* B Dudley-Ward			
	Fireman G Ewans			
	Traction Inspector K Treeby			
Weather:	Fine, sunny, dry			
Distance		**Schedule**	**Actual**	**Speeds**
Miles/Ch.	BRISTOL TEMPLE MEADS	0	0.00	*start*
8.02	Nailsea and Backwell	--	12.05	69
11.77	Yatton	--	15.25	59 *check*
16.60	Worle Jn.	20	19.57	62
19.53	*Uphill Jn.*	23	22.34	71
26.74	Highbridge	29	29.1	60
33.16	Bridgwater	37	34.55	*check*
40.19	*Cogload Jn.*	44	41.02	70
44.61	Taunton	49	45.55	20
47.01	SILK MILL LC	54	50.18	*stop*
9.46	*Whiteball tunnel (East)*	--	13.43	41
10.16	*Whiteball Summit*	--	14.55	42
14.66	Tiverton Parkway	18	19.12	82
21.09	*Hele and Bradnich*	--	23.56	84
29.38	EXETER St DAVIDS	34	32.01	*stop*
4.67	*Exminster*	--	7.46	68
10.42	Dawlish Warren	15	15.27	12 *check*
20.14	NEWTON ABBOT	32	33.25	*stop*
1.09	*MP 215 (Aller Jn.)*	--	3.16	29
3.73	*Dainton tunnel (East)*	--	8.44	28
8.67	Totnes	17	14.35	45
13.27	*MP 227/II Rattery*	--	22.44	36
17.76	*MP 232 Wrangaton*	--	28.24	49
21.05	Ivybridge	36	30.46	64
25.04	Hemerdon	41	36.07	46
29.69	PLYMOUTH NORTH ROAD	51	43.56	*stop*
1.20	Devonport	--	3.44	30
2.72	*St Budeaux*	6	6.31	31
4.18	Saltash	--	10.23	19
9.16	St Germans	19	17.20	33
14.53	Menheniot	--	25.41	54
17.58	Liskeard	33	30.00	44
21.08	Doublebois	--	35.20	47
22.73	*Largin*	41	37.58	44
28.75	Bodmin Parkway	--	43.16	31
30.26	Lostwithiel	53	48.55	40
34.61	PAR	65	64.39	*stop*

Table 8: 9 May 1998

uneventful, but it was clear that the excessive load was preventing the locomotive from ever getting into its stride to its optimum speed; instead, for almost 30min it just kept slogging its way sure-footedly up the 15 miles at speeds between 35 and 23 mph, with one injector on permanently taking the edge off the boiler pressure. Not what a 'King' was designed to do. There was a general sense of relief at the Garsdale water-stop and on the easier road thereafter the locomotive made up sufficient time to achieve a punctual arrival in Carlisle.

If anyone thought No 6024's visits to the northern fells hauling 520 tons would be a picnic, they were quickly put right. Unable to reach the speeds it required to have a sufficiently rapid draught through the fire for good steam generation, the climb was achieved with 160psi pressure by the engine's sheer strength and the Carlisle crew's finely judged nursing of the locomotive.

14 March 1998
Carlisle to Crewe via Appleby and Blackburn; 13 coaches; 157 miles; fine
Despite another excessive load, the locomotive wasn't perturbed by the tricky departure from Carlisle and the subsequent section to Appleby. However, an over-ambitious restart from Appleby depleted the boiler and eight miles into the climb shortage of steam and low boiler water level forced the crew to make an unscheduled stop at Kirby Stephen for a blow-up, rather than risk a stop in a more hostile position further up the climb. A sure restart was made and slow progress made to the top at Ais Gill but again the Garsdale water-stop couldn't arrive quickly enough. The climb of Whalley Bank was much more to the engine's liking and this tricky section was handled with particular ease. After Warrington the boiler was finding it increasingly difficult to steam and eventually on the approach to Crewe boiler pressure was again low and an undignified stop was forced on the crew for another blow-up.

This was another sobering experience. The reasons for the shortage of steam, however, were harder to define. Clearly, for the long climb, the load was excessive given the fundamental design of the locomotive. But there were other possible contributors, such as the effect of the new smokebox spark-arresting, crew unfamiliarity or an incipient mechanical problem that only came to light on the next run.

28 March 1998
Crewe to Carlisle via Blackburn and Hellifield; 13 coaches; 157 miles; fine, cloudy
This run was tainted by mechanical problems and was not the engine's finest hour! Some good running on the WCML was brought to a sudden

halt on the open line north of Weaver junction when the main reservoir pipe between the engine and tender leaked. The replacement was completed in only 12min and onto Blackburn all went well. Signals lost time to Hellifield (MP231) where it became clear that the locomotive wasn't steaming and there was a further delay while the fire was brought around. More stops were required at MP242 and MP246, evidence that the poor steaming was the result of a problem with the engine rather than for external reasons. After the late arrival at Carlisle the truth was revealed, with an impromptu fire in the smokebox clearly visible through a three-quarter inch gap between the smokebox door and its seal!

Obviously not only did this lack of a tight seal cause the steaming problems on this run but it had probably affected the steaming on the southbound run two weeks earlier; it was likely that the fault had been developing for some time.

4 April 1998

Carlisle to York via Appleby and Leeds; 13 coaches; 137 miles; fine, brief showers

With only a week between runs, emergency repairs were carried out to the smokebox door and the seal to the door-ring. Only the climb would reveal whether or not this work had done the trick. Another heavy load was handled well out of Carlisle and Appleby was made on time. This time the departure from Appleby was subdued and with 240psi boiler pressure the 'King' made steady, untroubled progress on the ascent at speeds between 32 and 45mph. The use of the second injector before Mallerstang, 13 miles into the climb, knocked the pressure and speed back, but there was still sufficient energy to keep the job going and Garsdale was achieved without incident. The train then proceeded to York and the engine enjoyed a couple of weeks in the limelight on the turntable in the NRM before making its way southwards light engine to Tyseley.

9 May 1998 *(Table 8)*

Bristol TM to Par; nine coaches; 162 miles; fine

After running light to Bristol from Tyseley No 6024 made the second unassisted run over the South Devon banks by steam in modern times and it also made the first recorded sortie by a 'King' into Cornwall over Brunel's famous bridge over the Tamar. These milestones were celebrated in grand style after the trials and tribulations in the north, with an average of 81mph between MPs 176 and 190 on the decent from Whiteball, including 85mph near Hele and an exciting 81mph near the foot of Hemerdon. More importantly, despite a standing start at Newport Abbot, the extra coach caused no problems to the performance of the locomotive on the climbs of Dainton and Rattery and in Cornwall. Without the demand for the sustained steaming rates experienced on the runs in the north, there was no obvious recurrence of the smokebox door problems and a punctual arrival at Par was achieved after a very fine run. The engine stabled at the delightful Bodmin & Wenford Railway for three weeks.

PAR to DIDCOT

Load:	9 coaches - 325 tons tare, 355 tons gross			
Crew:	*Driver* B Dudley-Ward			
	Fireman P Burns			
	Traction Inspector G Jones			
Weather:	Fine, sunny, dry			

Distance		*Schedule*	*Actual*	*Speeds*
Miles/Ch.	PAR	0	0.00	*start*
4.35	Lostwithiel	11	10.52	47
11.68	*Largin*	23	21.38	35
13.53	*Doublebois*	--	25.19	34
17.03	Liskeard	33	30.1	15 *check*
25.45	St Germans	42	40.32	59
30.43	Saltash	64	49.2	*sigs*
32.69	*St Budeaux*	72	52.41	46
34.61	PLYMOUTH NORTH ROAD	100	63.13	*stop*
4.00	*Plympton*	--	7.52	57
6.65	*Hemerdon*	18	12.45	21
10.56	Ivybridge	25	19.44	50
13.76	*MP 232 Wrangaton*	--	22.43	46
23.09	Totnes	39	32.19	63
27.72	*MP 218 (summit)*	--	37.58	30
30.67	*MP 215 (Aller Jn.)*	--	41.27	48 *brakes*
31.76	Newton Abbot	53	43.06	*sigs*
37.04	Teignmouth	--	49.29	61 *checks*
45.16	*Exminster*	--	67.23	73
52.03	EXETER St. DAVIDS	77	74.19	*stop*
1.20	*Cowley Bridge Jn.*	4	3.49	31
8.31	*Hele and Bradninch*	--	12.1	62
14.62	Tiverton Parkway	22	19.38	63
19.72	*MP 174 Whiteball Summit*	--	22.53	56
23.53	*Wellington*	--	26.06	84
25.72	*MP 168*	--	27.31	89
26.17	Bradford Crossing	--	27.53	86
30.60	Taunton	37	31.53	61
35.40	*Cogload Jn.*	42	35.51	76
42.25	Bridgwater	49	41.07	68
48.37	Highbridge	55	47.28	50 *check*
55.68	*Uphill Jn.*	65	55.11	71
58.61	*Worle Jn.*	70	59.32	45 *check*
63.44	Yatton	--	68.26	46
67.39	Nailsea and Backwell	--	72.51	56
73.47	Parson Street	87	79.56	27
75.39	BRISTOL TEMPLE MEADS	94	86.01	*stop*
4.43	Keynsham	--	9.23	53
11.4	BATH SPA	21	17.12	*stop*
10.61	*Thingley Jn.*	16	11.53	55
12.75	CHIPPENHAM	19	17.28	*stop*
10.69	*Wootton Bassett Jn.*	18	12.29	62
16.53	SWINDON	27	22.44	*stop*
10.64	*Uffington*	16	12.38	74
17.01	*Wantage Road*	--	17.37	78
24.13	DIDCOT	33	30.00	*stop*

30 May 1998 *(Table 9)*

Par to Didcot via Bristol TM; nine coaches; 228 miles; fine

The return run from Cornwall highlighted an impeccable piece of footplate work and timekeeping on an engine that had enjoyed some regular light work on the Bodmin & Wenford, so getting it nice and free in time

EXETER to PENZANCE

Load: 9 coaches - 329 tons tare, 355 tons gross
Crew: *Drivers B Dudley-Ward (to Plymouth), C Parry (to Penzance)*
Fireman G Ewans
Traction Inspector R Churchill
Weather: Fine, clear, sunny

Distance		Schedule	Actual	Speeds
Miles/Ch.	EXETER St DAVIDS	0	0.00	start
4.67	*Exminster*	--	7.34	62
10.42	Dawlish Warren	15	15.12	35/43
20.14	Newton Abbot	28	25.10	56
21.08	*MP 215 (Aller Jn.)*	--	26.09	57
23.71	*Dainton tunnel (East)*	36	29.35	34
28.74	Totnes	42	35.11	60
33.48	*MP 227/II Rattery*	--	41.55	40
38.08	*MP 232 Wrangaton*	--	47.09	55
40.35	Ivybridge	--	49.37	64
45.18	Hemerdon	--	54.27	57
52.04	PLYMOUTH NORTH ROAD	73	62.40 *sigs*	stop
1.20	Devonport	--	4.14	22
2.72	*St Budeaux*	--	6.48	47
4.20	Saltash	13	10.41	24
9.21	St Germans	--	17.04	33
14.53	Menheniot	--	24.39	62
17.63	Liskeard	37	28.16	27
21.05	Doublebois	--	33.11	46
22.73	*Largin*	--	35.43	47
26.75	Bodmin Parkway	--	40.06	47
30.28	Lostwithiel	56	42.16	57
34.58	Par	64	52.11	15
39.26	ST AUSTELL	72	62.26	stop
2.30	*Burngullow Jn.*	--	6.56	45
14.31	Truro	25	22.00	30
23.42	Redruth	--	35.58	36
27.14	Camborne	44	40.40	60
34.41	St. Erth	53	49.19	53
40.24	PENZANCE	63	58.26	stop

for this run. On the section between Plymouth and Newton Abbot the 'King' set the preservation bench-mark for the section at 43min 6sec without anyone really trying to break any records. The time for the short climb of Dainton westbound would not be bettered on any subsequent steam-hauled charter for three years. The engine was given its head between Exeter and Taunton and touched 90mph on Wellington bank. The run featured a mammoth turn of duty for Bryan Dudley-Ward, Paul Burns and Traction Inspector Gareth Jones, who stood on the footplate the entire journey to Didcot and having gained on the schedule on every section delivered a seven-minute early arrival. Again, the locomotive was wholly comfortable on home territory.

2 August 1998

Didcot to Worcester via Swindon and Cheltenham and return; 13 coaches; 176 miles; mild, hazy sun
Considering the load, this was a fine run by the locomotive after a competent run to Swindon. There followed good work up Sapperton from

Kemble although the descent was spoiled by an enforced stop due to an air-brake defect. After Cheltenham the train accelerated well and ran effortlessly near to its speed limit for a dozen miles or so. On the return the locomotive again cruised to Cheltenham and beyond Standish Junction was not pressed before Stroud. Then it was progressively opened up to a stirring blast on the bank from Chalford, a really excellent climb. This was the locomotive's first climb of Sapperton with 13 coaches.

22 August 1998

Newport to Carmarthen and return; 11 coaches; 173 miles; fine and sunny
This was another well judged run by the crews from Bristol Barton Hill and Newport, with a tense but successful restart on Cockett bank after being held at signals. Another excellent run overall with good punctuality on a load more suitable to the undulating South Wales road that was easily within the locomotive's capacity.

5 September 1998

Didcot to Weymouth via Reading, Castle Cary, Yeovil Pen Mill and return via Chippenham; 13 coaches; 249 miles; wet
This late-starting run was a very tough assignment for the locomotive and it became apparent quite early on that the exhaust beat was not quite right. Despite this, the engine persevered with some good, strong running up to Reading with a maximum of 71mph near Pangbourne and competent if unsensational work on the Berks & Hants' climbs. Restrained running down to Westbury conserved water and some time was clawed back during the station stop. The train was banked out of Weymouth and after Yeovil the running became more laboured, with a more pronounced blow from the exhaust. Nevertheless the Barton Hill crew nursed the locomotive along and delays were not excessive. On arrival back at Didcot, after inspection, a broken valve ring was diagnosed.

19 September 1998 *(Table 10)*

Exeter to Penzance; nine coaches; 132 miles; fine
This was the outbound run of a weekend tour involving 530 miles of main-line running. After emergency attention at Didcot the locomotive made a movement to the West Somerset Railway and spent nine days there. Then a light move to Exeter positioned the engine for this train. In glorious weather, despite slowing to avoid water carrying over at Starcross shortly after the start, the locomotive achieved its fastest time yet to the summit of Dainton bank and also on Rattery bank, with the always-consummate Bryan Dudley-Ward in charge. The time on the latter was to stand for four years against all-comers until beaten by No 6024 itself in 2002. There was another high-speed descent of Hemerdon, touching 82mph at MP242. To cap it all, the 37.5min it took from passing Newton Abbot to arrival at Plymouth North Road remains the fastest time with the permitted load on record.

Excellent running continued across Cornwall's wonderful railway, all viaducts and valleys, seen at its best on this fine day. It seemed that the

DIDCOT to YORK

Load: 11 coaches - 410 tons tare, 430 tons gross
Crew: *Drivers* A Roseblade (to Burton on Trent), N Hitch (to York)
Firemen A Bromley (to Burton on Trent), C Bayliss (to York)
Traction Inspectors B Dudley-Ward (to Burton on Trent), G Jones (to York)
Weather: Cold, intermittant sunshine and rain

Distance		Schedule	Actual	Speeds
Miles/Ch.	DIDCOT	0	0.00	*start*
5.25	Radley	6	4.33	49
10.31	Oxford	20	18.48	64
13.22	*Wolvercote Jn.*	24	21.26	65
22.11	Heyford	39	29.25	71
27.72	*Aynho Jn.*	47	34.28	70
29.45	Kings Sutton	--	35.53	70
33.06	BANBURY	51	42.18	*stop*
4.04	*Cropredy*	--	8.06	52
8.6	*Fenny Compton*	8	13.11	65
14.36	*Harbury Tunnel (north)*	--	17.57	72
19.71	Leamington Spa	--	23.00	33
21.64	Warwick	--	25.28	57
25.78	Hatton	--	30.00	52
30.15	Lapworth	--	34.13	58
32.59	DORRIDGE	34	48.01	*stop*
3.3	Solihull	--	7.48	53
9.74	LANDOR STREET Jn.	17	19.01	*stop*
6.08	Water Orton	8	9.40	25
11.23	Kingsbury Jn.	19	23.45	16
17.04	Tamworth HL	25	33.43	56
29.65	Burton on Trent	44	48.38	*stop*
36.12	Stenson Jn.	52	57.22	57
40.76	Derby	61	66.03	*stop*
50.69	Ambergate Jn.	--	79.18	55
60.77	Clay Cross South Jn.	82	90.18	63
67.63	BARROW HILL SOUTH Jn.	93	99.58	*stop*
15.67	Aldwarke Jn.	23	22.22	63
25.54	Moorthorpe	35	32.49	52
32.52	PONTEFRACT BAGHILL	44	41.34	*stop*
6.29	Milford	10	12.26	32
10.42	Church Fenton	16	17.28	54
21.2	YORK	30	31.30	*stop*

Table 11: 14 November 1998

LEEDS to LONDON KINGS CROSS

Load: 13 coaches (+ Class 86/2) - 573 tons tare, 590 tons gross
Crew: *Drivers* W Wilkinson (to Retford), D Davies (to Kings Cross)
Firemen M Joyce (to Retford), C Greystone (to Kings Cross)
Traction Inspectors J Smith (to Retford), B Dudley-Ward (to Kings Cross)
Weather: Cold, wet at first, overcast

Distance		Schedule	Actual	Speeds
Miles/Ch.	LEEDS	0	0.00	*start*
9.78	Wakefield Westgate	19	21.30	36/28
19.69	*South Kirby Jn.*	33	33.48	75
24.78	Aldwick Jn.	40	37.42	78
29.66	Doncaster	45	41.54	54
33.63	*Loversall Carr Jn.*	68	45.47	63
47.14	RETFORD	89	63.05	*stop*
18.41	Newark Northgate	37	22.16	71
28.73	*Barkston South Jn.*	48	32.10	55
33.11	Grantham	53	39.18	17 *slow line*
36.59	HIGH DYKE UP LOOP	61	50.17	*stop*
0.70	*MP 101*	--	4.14	30 *fast line*
1.63	*Stoke Summit*	4	5.51	35
2.70	*MP 99*	--	--	56
3.70	*MP 98*	--	--	60
6.70	*MP 95*	--	--	76
8.70	*MP 93*	--	--	83
9.70	*MP 92*	--	--	84
13.18	*Essendine*	--	15.40	78
17.06	*Tallington*	20	21.36	27 *slow line*
25.41	PETERBOROUGH	30	37.01	*stop*
9.57	CONNINGTON LOOP	13	22.28	*stop*
7.62	Huntingdon	13	19.21	39
22.42	Sandy	28	36.16	54
34.58	Hitchin	40	52.58	32
39.05	STEVENAGE	47	64.21	*stop*
7.20	Welwyn Garden City	15	11.56	51
14.68	Potters Bar	25	21.26	36
22.47	Alexandra Palace	35	31.12	50
25.04	Finsbury Park	41	38.38	34
27.45	KINGS CROSS	50	46.01	*stop*

entire population of Cornwall came out to see the engine make its way to Penzance. All went well with a triumphant entry into Penzance station and the engine was then towed in reverse to St Blazey for servicing and stabling overnight.

20 September 1998

Falmouth to Swindon via Bristol TM; nine coaches; 234 miles; fine
Next day, a complicated movement from St Blazey positioned the locomotive in Falmouth for the return when again the crowds were enormous. The late arrival of the stock unfortunately seemed to set the tone because the running was subdued for most of the time and featured some thoroughly underwhelming work over the South Devon banks, with Hemerdon being particularly disappointing. The engine was due to come

off at Bristol before the train returned to Gloucester, but the late arrival of the stock had set the timings back and on arrival at Bristol it transpired that an engineering possession north of Westerleigh Junction meant the train had to be diverted via Bath and Kemble. So the 'King' remained on the front until Swindon. This was another run free of mechanical troubles.

14 November 1998 *(Table 11)*

Didcot to York via Derby and Chesterfield; 11 coaches; 197 miles; cloudy, wet
This was another new route for a 'King' north of Derby and positioned the locomotive for another week's stay at the NRM before a special railtour. The first half of the day featured some good, consistent speed with some lively work up from Banbury, including almost 80mph at Fosse Road and a superb climb of Hatton bank, but checks frustrated progress from Birmingham to Derby with a few minutes lost along the way. Thereafter, the rather disjointed route prevented much excitement apart from a good 71mph before Swinton but arrival in York was punctual.

a failed tanker pump to get the engine watered. With paths at a premium on this busy main line, a further delay added to the lateness and departure from Retford was eventually 56min late. More spirited work reduced the delay by 13min at Grantham but subsequent signal delays decayed the gain and despite a heartening 84mph on Stoke bank — this was a huge effort after the standing start from the scheduled stop at High Dyke — the arrival at Connington Loop for water was back to 56min down.

Due to the hard steaming involved in trying to make up the lost time with this excessive load, the tender was completely empty by Connington. To add insult to injury, it transpired that the driver of the Class 86 had baled out at the scheduled stop at Peterborough! With another 77 miles to go to King's Cross and no more opportunities for water, the tender had to be filled completely. Ludicrously, at the moment when the 'insurance' might actually be called upon, the Class 86 had no driver! There was no choice but to drive the locomotive very conservatively thereafter and, combined with an increasingly reluctant fire, the remainder of the run was unexciting and arrival at King's Cross was 99min late.

Although not a first for a 'King', this was an interesting if complex run, although it came as no surprise to discover that the ECML is a very different place from the steam-friendly environment of 1948. By contrast with the logistical fiasco, the loco performed admirably and none of the lost time could be attributed to it.

20 December 1998

Kings Cross to Norwich and return via Cambridge; 13 coaches + Class 47; 255 miles; cold, fine

It was difficult to believe a 'King' was leaving King's Cross for Norwich! The climb out of King's Cross through Gasworks Tunnel was of no real consequence to the locomotive as it was given a push by the Class 47 that had towed the train in from Bounds Green and which stayed attached all day. The 'King' produced some bright and noisy running throughout the run with 80mph shortly before Norwich but, having suffered a series of checks at regular intervals, it was beyond the Acton crew to make up time and arrival in Norwich was 18min late. The welcome at the destination was a very warming aspect of the day.

The final run of 1998 to a completely unfamiliar destination summed up the varied challenges the locomotive had handled in 1998. Completing almost 4,000 miles in the 12 months the locomotive had traversed the country and had travelled to York and Weymouth, Carlisle and Penzance, King's Cross and Carmarthen. The runs in the Northern Fells had revealed some limitations with the locomotive, which came as no surprise, and also some defects, which achieved unwelcome notoriety, but despite these disappointments, there were also some high spots. Importantly, the locomotive had stood up to some extremely arduous work involving heavy loads; indeed, far heavier than many thought advisable.

1999 was to prove another year of work away from home as well as visits to familiar territory and again performance in the early part of the year

2 November 1998 *(Table 12)*

Leeds to Kings Cross; 13 coaches + Class 86; 185 miles; damp, cold

During the 1948 Locomotive Exchanges, gauging prevented 'Kings' working anywhere away from home territory apart from the Eastern Region. For a couple of weeks, No 6018 *King Henry VI* had worked between King's Cross and Leeds and this rail-tour was planned to celebrate the 50th anniversary of these workings. Wearing No 6018's number and nameplates the engine was piloted light from York and after a delay due to the stock's late arrival, left Leeds with its half-full train and a dead Class 86 electric locomotive on the rear, 'for insurance'. Apart from raising the load to an absurd 590 tons, the 'insurance' was not called upon as the day progressed and caused more problems than it solved.

Despite this excessive weight, the 'King' made an energetic climb out of Leeds and a lively run to Doncaster before storming along the ECML to the Retford water-stop, having converted the 18min late departure into a seven-minute early arrival. There, the train-length first caused problems by blocking the line at the rear and lost all the gained time and then nothing short of a farce unfolded as the water-tanker driver, support crew, local Fire Brigade and all and sundry tried to sort out incompatible hose fittings and

proved to be mixed. However, after a long period of untroubled running a freak event happened in September, which set the locomotive back many months and caused a considerable crisis. Having completed its work into and out of King's Cross, in late December 1998 the locomotive returned to Didcot and then in January 1999 made its way northwards again, to Crewe.

1999

23 January 1999

Crewe to Holyhead and return; 13 coaches; 211 miles; very cold, grey, strong prevailing wind followed by drizzle

A day that was run to assist to raise funds for the reopening of the branch from Gaerwen Junction to Amlwch began with much promise but was destined to end in frustration. A poorly-filled train of 13 coaches was burdened with a slack schedule on the outbound, a tight schedule on the return and an imposed restriction of 65mph line speed throughout, punctuated by regular checks along the way. An early arrival at Llandudno Junction was achieved without too much bother but a joint in the air-pump blew which had to be operated intermittently rather than continuously. The regular need to accelerate and brake this heavy train resulted in an arrival in Holyhead a few minutes down.

The pump was repaired during the layover but delayed departure for the return by 30min. Even without this, the notion that the schedule could be kept was sheer fantasy, and unsurprisingly, with progress being constantly checked, arrival back in Crewe was 88min down.

14 February 1999

Paddington to Salisbury via Westbury and Basingstoke; 11 coaches; 207 miles; fine

This was an excursion into uncharted waters, but featured an exciting climb to Savernake summit and a thunderous ascent of the bank out of Westbury to Warminster. A broken pressure-gauge feed-pipe caused a headache for the footplate crew after Basingstoke and the run back was relatively subdued. Arrival back in Paddington was achieved without other problems.

6 March 1999

Crewe to Holyhead and return via Llandudno Junction; 13 coaches; 211 miles; mainly cold drizzle, some dry intervals.

The locomotive made a return visit to Holyhead only six weeks after its first-ever run there and made a much better stab at the route than it was allowed before. Still constrained by a maximum line speed of 65mph the run featured some rapid acceleration from Crewe and Holyhead and a late departure on the return was converted into an early arrival back in Crewe.

26 March 1999 *(Table 13)*

Crewe to Carlisle and return via Preston; 12 coaches; 282 miles; fine at first, wet later.

CREWE to CARLISLE via PRESTON and return

Table 13: 26 March 1999

Load: 12 coaches - 447 tons tare, 482 tons gross
Crew: Drivers B Morrison/R Hatton (to Carlisle), G Hodgson (to Crewe)
Firemen R Hatton/B Morrison (to Carlisle), P Kane (to Crewe)
Traction Inspectors P Davies (to Carlisle), J McCabe (to Crewe)
Weather: Dry, fine at first, later overcast and showers

Distance Miles/Ch.		Schedule	Actual	Speeds
	CREWE	0	0.00	start
8.80	Winsford Jn.	14.30	11.42	70
24.15	Warrington	30.30	26.31	69
27.50	Winwick Jn.	33.30	29.21	69
35.90	Wigan	42	37.24	64
47.00	Leyland	--	47.56	80
51.00	Preston	64	52.14	13
55.65	BARTON DOWN LOOP	75	62.12	stop
16.30	Lancaster	19	18.22	--
18.22	Morecombe South Jn.	21	20.01	67
22.38	Carnforth North Jn.	25	25.03	64
37.30	Oxenholme	40.30	39.49	20
48.10	Tebay	59	77.13	44
50.30	MP 34	--	raise steam	stop
51.30	MP 35	--	107.20	15
52.30	MP 36	--	111.03	15
53.30	MP 37	--	116.46	11
54.10	MP 37/III Shap summit (N)	--	120.39	19
67.36	PENRITH	89	139.34	stop
18.03	CARLISLE	25	22.35	stop
0.00	CARLISLE	0	0.00	start
9.09	MP 60	--	15.03	55
14.09	MP 55	--	20.29	60
17.69	Penrith	28	24.20	61
19.09	MP 50	--	25.32	63
24.09	MP 45	--	31.12	46
29.09	MP 40	--	37.53	47
31.49	MP 37/II Shap summit (S)	--	40.53	54
34.09	MP 35	--	43.07	73
37.29	Tebay	54	45.52	72
44.09	MP 25	--	52.04	72
50.01	Oxenholme	67	57.11	66
54.09	MP 15	--	60.36	74
63.15	CARNFORTH U & D LOOP	82	73.25	stop
4.02	Morecombe South Jn.	5	7.48	28 sigs
5.74	Lancaster	8	11.02	45 sigs
26.74	PRESTON	37	34.53	stop
4.00	Leyland	--	7.09	46
15.10	Wigan	21	22.04	60 sigs
23.50	Winwick Jn.	29.30	47.04	63 sigs
26.85	Warrington	34.30	50.09	67
42.20	Winsford Jn.	55	69.11	51
51.00	CREWE	67	85.04	stop

Few people who travelled on this train will ever forget it. On the face of it, four miles of Shap's 1 in 75 should have been well within the capability of the 'King' but the load was a concern. Moreover, a series of circumstances contrived to undo the meticulous plans that had been laid for the run. Colombian coal had been the brand of choice for a little while and, though on recent runs the fire had tended to get dirty, if the fire was regularly cleaned, the coal burned well and not too fast, generating plenty of heat; in a number of ways it replicated the now-unobtainable

26 March 1999 — Racing towards Penrith on the southbound climb to Shap summit soon after departure from Carlisle for Preston and Crewe. *John Cooper-Smith*

best that could be achieved. Just to make matters worse, a Railtrack representative confronted the driver with his speed limit breach through Leyland; the driver retorted that the 'King' was incapable of anything more than 70mph! This was to have repercussions later.

Some time was gained at the stop and when the water was in and the fire brightened up somewhat, the locomotive was ready to get going with the chance of saving some time. Then the train was held for 16 more minutes for a service train. In the end the departure was still 61min down. Progress along the flat to Carnforth was reasonable but on the climb immediately following it became very pedestrian and, once onto Grayrigg bank, was at best laboured with the effort steadily wilting. Digging in deep and with boiler pressure down to 120psi, the train eventually crawled over the top, with the respite of the loop at either Grayrigg or Tebay available. By now the boiler had rallied to 160psi and, fearing the refusal of another path, the footplate crew decided to press on. However, unsurprisingly the effort though better, wasn't enough and at MP34, about a mile onto the 1 in 75 the train came to its inevitable stand.

Now, without any alternative, the long fire-irons were unlocked and used to make some improvement in the firebox. Almost four hours after it was first made, the fire saw some effective cleaning action for the first time! Despite a couple of episodes of heavy slipping, the engine wrestled its train up to Shap and over the top. Arrival in Carlisle was over 100min late after what must have been the slowest ascent in preservation.

The servicing at Upperby was to say the least, an eye-opener! While the fire was shovelled out and remade and new coal was loaded, unburned char was removed from the smokebox; two-thirds of the height of the smokebox door and right back to the tube-plate, it took two support crewmen 45min to remove it all. When the engine returned to the platform eventually, the train left Carlisle 95min late. Passengers were then provided with one of the most dramatic ever 45min of main-line steam. In the hands of Gordon Hodgson and Paul Kane, the revitalised 'King' progressively got to grips with its task. With the necessary precision and *finesse* these two fine enginemen began to press the engine, gently at first but with increasing energy and its eventual rampage through Penrith and beyond to the summit 31 miles from the start was later established as one of the longest periods of sustained steaming by a 'King' in service ever recorded and probably the fastest southbound ascent of Shap by any 4-6-0 with such a load.

Unsurprisingly towards the end of this 282-mile marathon, again without the necessary cleaning of the fire, the steaming deteriorated and the run was completed in a subdued way rather than with a flourish, with coal a long way back in the tender and water low. Arguably the locomotive had, in a single day, memorably registered both its most difficult moment and also its most magnificent.

27 March 1999

Chester to Newport via Shrewsbury; 13 coaches; 137 miles; fine

Those who stayed with the locomotive for this next run on the following day found themselves embroiled in a completely unexpected slice of fall-

high-calorific soft Welsh coal which traditionally best-suited the locomotive's firebox. So, with a full tender and more waiting at Carlisle, it appeared everything had been done for this high-profile run by the 'King'.

Don't you believe it! Just as the locomotive was ready to leave the depot with the fire ready for an on-time departure, news came that the stock would be an over hour late into Crewe. With the locomotive safely sitting in an adjoining platform under the 25kV overhead wires, with 250psi in the boiler and a thick but cooling fire, the stock eventually arrived and the 482-ton train duly departed 76min late. There then followed an extraordinary passage of hard running at the hands of the Crewe men, punctuated by easing for signals, all of which was accompanied by copious quantities of black exhaust. Thus progress was made for over 50 miles, culminating in 83mph after Leyland, shortly before the first water-stop at Barton Loop.

With the firebox containing a large fire with a dull orange hue and a correspondingly heavy coal usage evident, attempts were made to return the fire to life. It desperately needed sorting out having been under the wires for well over two hours, but the long fire-irons, in accordance with standard practice, were locked away. So using the short fire-irons was the

out resulting from the speeding incident the day before and overnight spent hours debating with Railtrack and EWS the locomotive's fitness — or otherwise — to run. The Crewe driver, who had in effect cleared himself of all blame for his speed through Leyland, left the authorities no choice but to scrutinise the locomotive and particularly its speedometer. Their position was that the speedometer's accuracy must be proved before the locomotive returned to the network. After continual negotiation through the early hours the *impasse* was eventually overcome and it was agreed that the locomotive would be piloted to Chester by a Class 66 and its speedometer visually compared with that on the diesel. If accurate the train could run, if not the locomotive would stay marooned at Chester. Needless to say the two speedos corresponded exactly!

It came as a relief to all to get coupled up to this train and make a start. A stirring climb up Gresford bank cheered everyone up and the locomotive performed well for most of the day. However, it was again tending towards shortness of steam after a few hours, this time on the climb of Llanvihangel bank north of Abergavenny.

1 May 1999

Didcot Circular via Kemble, Worcester and Oxford; 12 coaches; 157 miles; fine, sunny

The engine performed well with some excellent running throughout the day. It was notable for being probably the first time the 'King' was seen hauling a set of green Mark 1 coaches.

5 June 1999 *(Table 14)*

Acton Wells to Bristol TM, return to Didcot; 13 coaches; 180 miles; not recorded

Considering the load this run featured some sensational running for most of the day, with punctual time-keeping at station-stops. Signal checks ruined the running to Reading but thereafter there followed some better running. The arrival back in Didcot only one minute down left everyone feeling they had had a good day.

3 July 1999

Port Talbot to Fishguard via Carmarthen, return to Newport; 10 coaches; 217 miles; fine

This was another run with an unusual destination — and unique for a 'King' — and where, on the day its success was dependent on improvisation. The steam section was scheduled to start at Newport but due to the stock's diesel failing, No 6024 and its coach moved onto the first water-stop to save time. Departure was still 53min late and with some unspectacular running along the Swansea Avoiding line this lateness was maintained to Carmarthen where the loco was turned and attached to the rear of the train to be diesel-hauled in reverse to Fishguard at 35mph! Huge crowds turned out for this 'first' so the departure was taken easily up the bank for safety reasons but thereafter the running was exciting and noisy and most passengers were left feeling at the end that the rather

ACTON WELLS to BRISTOL TEMPLE MEADS, return to DIDCOT

Load: 13 coaches - 477 tons tare, 510 tons gross
Crew: *Drivers* D Davies (to Bristol), P Burns (to Didcot)
Firemen C Greystone (to Bristol), G Ewans (to Didcot)
Traction Inspectors D Donovan (to Bristol), B Dudley-Ward (to Didcot)
Weather: Not recorded

Distance		Schedule	Actual	Speeds
Miles/Ch.	ACTON WELLS	0	0.00	*start*
2.54	Ealing Broadway	--	9.08	39
6.04	Southall	17	13.23	41
15.34	Slough	36	24.02	32
21.17	Maidenhead	43	31.52	30
27.79	Twyford	49	39.06	68
32.76	READING	57	46.31	*stop*
5.45	Pangbourne	--	7.12	67
8.62	Goring & Streatley	--	9.58	73
12.39	Cholsey & Moulsford	--	12.56	76
17.12	DIDCOT PARKWAY	20	18.30	*stop*
0.35	DIDCOT WEST END	2	2.36	*stop*
6.57	Wantage Road	12	13.50	43
10.18	CHALLOW	18	22.29	*stop*
2.56	Uffington	6	5.08	57
13.40	Swindon	19	15.26	62
19.09	*Wootton Bassett Jn.*	24	20.16	76
21.17	*MP 85*	--	21.54	78
22.17	*MP 86*	--	22.40	80
23.17	*MP 87*	--	23.23	86
24.17	*MP 88*	--	24.06	83
30.13	Chippenham	34	28.41	75
32.26	*Thingley Jn.*	--	30.27	72
35.29	*Box Tunnel (East)*	--	32.59	42
43.08	BATH SPA	49	44.06	*stop*
6.72	Keynsham	--	8.43	56
11.40	BRISTOL TEMPLE MEADS	20	21.00	*stop*
0.00	BRISTOL TEMPLE MEADS	0	0.00	*start*
11.40	BATH SPA	18	16.08	*stop*
10.62	*Thingley Jn.*	14	14.53	62
12.75	Chippenham	16	16.53	67
23.79	*Wootton Bassett Jn.*	25	27.02	63
29.48	Swindon	31	33.20	48
40.40	*Uffington*	42	42.51	76
42.71	*Challow*	45	45.03	60
46.49	*Wantage Road*	54	54.01	15 *sigs*
53.40	DIDCOT WEST END	66	64.55	*stop*

quirky itinerary had been worthwhile. This was another good outing for the locomotive with a relatively easy load.

1 August 1999

Didcot to Kingswear via Bristol TM; 12 coaches; 169 miles; fine, hot

This was a run of two contrasting parts, with some lively running to Swindon which continued to Bristol, including 84mph down Dauntsey bank, followed by some sustained good work as far as Bridgwater. But then steam pressure deteriorated. The water stop at Silk Mill offered temporary respite but, after the departure, boiler pressure and water level caused concern again and were adjudged to be too low just short of Whiteball tunnel, where the crew decided to stop. An unfussy restart was made on the 1 in 80 and the train made a brisk run down to Exeter.

PAIGNTON to BRISTOL TEMPLE MEADS

Load: 11 coaches - 401 tons tare, 420 tons gross
Crew: *Driver* P Burns
       Fireman G Ewans
       Traction Inspector B Dudley-Ward
Weather: Dry, fine, hazy sunshine

Distance		Schedule	Actual	Speeds
Miles/Ch.	PAIGNTON	0	0.00	start
2.13	Torquay	--	5.33	42
7.03	*MP 215 Aller Jn.*	--	13.27	37
8.07	Newton Abbot	18	15.14	30
13.19	Teignmouth	--	21.40	56
17.58	Dawlish Warren	31	26.30	64
21.42	*Powderham Crossing*	--	29.46	74
26.60	*City Basin Jn.*	--	34.14	60
28.20	EXETER St. DAVIDS	45	37.59	stop
1.20	*Cowley Bridge Jn.*	4	3.43	41
3.56	*Stoke Canon*	--	6.41	57
9.72	*MP 184*	--	12.32	70
10.72	*MP 183*	--	13.23	70
11.72	*MP 182*	--	14.14	70
12.45	*Collompton*	--	14.48	70
16.46	Tiverton Parkway	23	18.18	70
19.72	*MP 174 Whiteball Summit*	--	21.22	59
20.09	*Whiteball tunnel (West)*	--	21.35	61
20.59	*Whiteball tunnel (East)*	--	22.09	70
21.72	*MP 172*	--	23.07	75
22.72	*MP 171*	--	23.54	80
23.52	*Wellington*	--	24.29	77
26.20	*Bradford Crossing*	--	26.38	69
26.72	*MP 167*	--	27.14	69
29.37	Silk Mill Crossing	--	29.22	74
30.61	Taunton	39	30.24	76
35.49	*Cogload Jn.*	44	34.17	75
42.25	Bridgwater	50	39.35	75
48.47	Highbridge	--	44.28	78
55.68	*Uphill Jn.*	64	50.12	74
58.61	*Worle Jn.*	--	53.08 *sigs*	37
63.44	Yatton	--	63.39	29
67.39	Nailsea and Backwell	--	70.41	34
73.57	Parson Street	86	86.51	18
75.41	BRISTOL TEMPLE MEADS	92	91.39	stop

Station delays due to an attempted suicide added to the time already lost and more time was lost at Paignton.

A misjudgement of the load by the P&DSR crew up to Churston further delayed matters when another blow-up was needed and arrival in Kingswear was 57min late. Although this was a heavy load, it was not outside the capacity of the locomotive, so the steaming problems were again of concern especially as this was on home territory. One benefit of the run in the fine weather proved that the spark-arresting had prevented any chance of setting fire to the parched undergrowth.

5 September 1999 *(Table 15)*
Paignton to Gloucester via Bristol TM; 11 coaches; 142 miles; fine
This run more than any other typified the spectrum of feelings about operating a locomotive on the main line and was detrimentally to influence the

story of the locomotive for the next six months. Many felt it summed up the highs and lows of 1998 and 1999. The engine had stayed on the P&DSR for over a month in service and was thoroughly free-running. The run was planned to go to Birmingham to position it for work in the Midlands. All started well and with a relatively light train, good times on the non-stop section from Exeter to Bristol were hoped for. And these hopes were justified at first. A slightly late departure from Paignton was converted into an early arrival at St David's and, after watering, we left only half a minute late. There then followed a sustained storm of the climb up to Whiteball which was as good as anything seen by a GW locomotive before and, despite strict adherence to speed limits, the train passed Taunton eight minutes early, in 30min 24sec for the 30.8 miles, which was then the fastest time in preservation.

The running after Taunton was continued in like vein; for the 35 miles from Whiteball tunnel the train averaged 75mph to Uphill Junction, at which point the train was running 13min early. Signals brought an end to this dramatic dash to let a Weston-super-Mare service train to run ahead. Clear once more after Worle Junction, the regulator was opened again but a loud bang combined with flying debris announced that the engine was in major mechanical trouble. After a hasty assessment the crippled locomotive toiled along the flat road and onto Bristol where it was declared a failure. Fortunately the early running provided plenty of grace and the train was still on time at Bristol.

A Class 47 was hastily procured to pilot the engine and train to Gloucester as it was agreed that Horfield bank would be too much for the 'King' unassisted. At Gloucester the locomotive swapped with LMS '8F' No 48773 from the Severn Valley and the 'King' was towed to Tyseley by the Class 47 for repairs. It transpired that, on opening the regulator at Worle Junction, water had 'carried over' and the right-hand inside valve-head had disintegrated causing serious damage to the valve and valve rings.

10 October 1999
Tyseley to Worcester and Stratford Upon Avon and return; five coaches; 114 miles; cold, dry, fine
This run formed a 'running-in' turn for the locomotive after its valve repairs necessary following the unfortunate failure on the last run.

13 November 1999
Stratford-upon-Avon to Weymouth via Reading, Andover and Southampton; 11 coaches + Class 33; 226 miles; dull, damp
This run confirmed that following the valve repairs, the locomotive was still not fully recovered. The start from Stratford was adequate but throughout the day performance deteriorated in inverse proportion to coal and water consumption and it became clear that things were far from right in the steam chests. An incessant chimney 'blow' indicated a valve or valves not closing properly, confirmed by a ravenous fire causing a towering black exhaust. The continuous draught was so severe that by

the Oxford stop the tender was half-empty as a result of almost unbroken firing.

The suspicion had also existed before the run that the smokebox door still had a leak with its seat in the door-ring which was allowing air in, distorting the draught and hampering steaming. In the days preceding this run some repairs had been attempted but it appeared that this only made matters worse. The unchecked draught caused by a broken valve constantly drew air in through the defective door seal, igniting the smokebox char and created enormous heat in the smokebox. The door was so badly warped it had to be written off after this run.

The smokebox was emptied at Oxford and extra coal ordered for the servicing stop at Andover but time was lost steadily throughout the day; this was magnified by the failure of the water–delivery pump at Andover. With increasing signs of distress the engine eventually succumbed after stopping for signals on an incline west of Bournemouth and the train thereafter was powered by the Class 33 at the rear.

So ended 1999, a sorry story indeed. Paradoxically, with the exception of the valve ring problem in September 1998, the locomotive had enjoyed 18 months free of any mechanical trouble until the incident at Worle Junction in September 1999, so despite that setback, there had been a lot of good reliable work in the year with well over 3,000 miles covered. The locomotive stabled at the Yeovil Steam Centre for over three months from 13 November 1999 until early March 2000, during which period an intensive programme of repairs to all the areas causing concerns was initiated. All the valves were removed, stripped down and inspected, identifying that both right-hand inside valve-heads had sustained damage. Some valve components had disappeared completely. The view was that this was a result of residual debris from the incident at Worle Junction in September. The smokebox door and the ring which attached it to the boiler barrel were removed, scrapped and replaced with new. The smokebox spark-arresting screens were modified to assist the free-flow of gases to return the draughting to its original level before 1998.

Unsurprisingly, the locomotive was quarantined until Railtrack was satisfied about its mechanical reliability. On completion of its repairs, the locomotive was permitted to run light to the West Somerset Railway for bedding in the new valves for a few days. It was then piloted to Southall via the Berks & Hants by a Class 66. Further work on the main line was dependent upon a satisfactory loaded test train which duly ran in mid-March 2000 from Southall to Didcot and back, fortunately without problems and the locomotive returned to the main line with a clean bill of health.

2000

18 March 2000
London Victoria to Taunton (WSR) via Swindon and Westbury; 13 coaches; 167 miles; cold, dry, fine
This was the first-ever departure of a 'King' from Victoria. Fit again, this

5 September 1999 — Passing Shaldon Bridge, Teignmouth, in morning mist, shortly after starting an eventful day on a special from Paignton to Birmingham.
Richard Jones

was a good run for the engine to prove that it was back to its usual self and began a stable period of lively work that was mechanically trouble-free on the main line and private lines, so winning back enthusiast friends and rail-tour promoters. When the opportunity offered some fast running was achieved, particularly between Castle Cary and Cogload Junction. The return to the West Somerset Railway allowed plenty of low-stress work, to the engine's benefit. Time-keeping was generally good and allowed an on-time arrival in Bishop's Lydeard where 'Manor' No 7820 *Dinmore Manor* was attached as pilot engine to Minehead.

17 May 2000
Exeter to Didcot via Frome and Reading; 13 coaches; 154 miles; fine
The original plan was to start this rail-tour from Taunton facing west and go via Exeter Central, Honiton and Yeovil to Castle Cary and onto the Berks & Hants. A last-minute panic over bridge clearances changed all that so there was no choice but to make a light engine move from the WSR to Plymouth to turn and then return to Exeter to take on the train. Overall the locomotive put on another lively show with a heavy train over a classic route and it confirmed that the engine had overcome all its mechanical problems. There was no recurrence of valve problems and the new smokebox door and the modifications to the spark-arresting had sorted out the smokebox so steaming was much more reliable.

12 March 2000 — Shortly after arrival at the Southall Steam Centre being prepared for the next rail-tour. *Kevin Blake*

a light engine move was made to York in August. This sell-out run took place without incident, with the locomotive yet again being seen in new territory for part of the route. An energetic thrash up the ECML to Doncaster was another first for the 'King' and the locomotive kept time against a very tight schedule after Doncaster. Water supply problems at Barrow Hill lost the scheduled path but the engine was allowed to stretch its legs on the Midland main line and pulled back some time so the arrival at Peterborough was only a few minutes down.

7 October 2000

Paddington to Gloucester via Swindon and Kemble and return; 12 coaches; 228 miles; dry, fine

This run featured some high quality running all day with excellent time-keeping, with the locomotive shared between EWS crews from Acton, Didcot, Bristol Barton Hill and Newport. The highlights were the secure climb of Sapperton to Kemble and then a dramatic passage of the 24 miles from Swindon to Didcot in only 26min start to stop. Arrival in Paddington was 13min early.

25 November 2000

Taunton to Plymouth and return to Westbury; 13 coaches; 209 miles; cold, dull, rain

The run was double-headed with GWR 'Hall' class No 4936 *Kinlet Hall* and ran in the aftermath of the Hatfield crash, when many service trains had been cancelled and the network was peppered with temporary speed restrictions. These rather spoiled the smooth-running of the day and were often unhelpfully located. Working throughout the day in vacuum brake mode the engine performed faultlessly but, after converting to air at Exeter following the detachment of the 'Hall', the air compressor failed on the open line at Stoke Canon and the whole train had to be converted back to vacuum.

9 December 2000

Banbury to Birmingham International; 12 coaches; 40 miles; dry

This run was arranged in order to get the locomotive located at Crewe for a return match with the S&C, but the whole thing was torpedoed by the air pump again, forcing the job to be run in vacuum braking mode and as a consequence the removal of the air-braked generator car before the start. Some fairly uninspired running was terminated at Birmingham International where the AWS packed up. This one was best forgotten.

The year's activities were severely truncated by the repairs in the early part and the natural resistance on the part of promoters to hire the loco. The Hatfield crash made matters difficult for everyone and created a sense of uncertainty all round, particularly with passengers. This was reflected for some considerable time and the first run of 2001 was to turn out to be the only surviving leg of an ambitious programme which planned to take the rehabilitated locomotive around the north of England and into Scotland.

Although an over-enthusiastic departure from Exeter depleted the boiler on the lower slopes, the climb to Whiteball summit and the tunnel beyond was respectable and the train touched 81mph at Wellington. The locomotive sustained very good effort on the tough bank to Brewham. It was handled more gently up to Savernake but flew down the slope to Newbury, completing 18 miles at an average of 73mph. Arrival at Didcot was on time and the locomotive was back to being economical in its use of coal and water despite delivering some considerable power outputs at times during the day.

20 May 2000

Bristol TM to Didcot; 13 coaches; 64 miles; fine

This was a short run and went well, with the engine well in control of its load.

16 September 2000

York to Peterborough via Barrow Hill and Melton Mowbray; 13 coaches; 150 miles; fine

After a spell at Didcot, when essential routine maintenance was caught up,

2001

10 February 2001

Carlisle to Crewe via Blackburn; 13 coaches; 167 miles; heavy rain, strong winds

A light engine move on the WCML took the engine to Carlisle to renew battle with the S&C. The promoter yet again put an excessive load behind the 'King'. This time, post-Hatfield, the southbound S&C was littered with 20mph temporary speed restrictions so it was almost inevitable that recovery from each of these would be problematic for the 'King'. A 26min late start from Carlisle was followed by some energetic work to Appleby. Still late by the same margin, the start from the Appleby stop was very quick and this appeared to work this time, the extra momentum carrying the train a good way into the climb. However, the constant need for acceleration followed by easing for the restrictions took their toll and with the boiler low on water the crew brought the engine to a stand just short of the summit in order to top up. Still in torrential rain which probably would have undone most Pacifics, the locomotive made a very slippery climb of Whalley bank but due to fine handling by Gordon Hodgson, eventually defeated this tricky low-speed climb of 1 in 82.

Although some of the lateness was regained before the stop at Blackburn the whole enterprise was finally undone by the time it took to water and departure was 38min late. To make matters worse, as soon as the locomotive accelerated away from the stop, the chimney exhaust made it plain that the boiler was priming. As boiler levels were not excessive, there had to be an external explanation for this sudden development. With real concerns for the integrity of the valves, the footplate crew was requested to take it easy for the remainder of the run and Crewe was reached without causing valve damage. Analysis of the water following the run revealed that the load taken at Blackburn contained a detergent, apparently used to flush out the road tanker.

14 April 2001

Bristol to Kingswear, return to Taunton (WSR); 12 coaches; 162 miles; fine

This train carried a special headboard as a memorial to Bryan Williams, a supporter of No 6024 and a professional railway planner. Bryan's knowledge of Western lines and scheduling had been legendary. The run yet again featured some strong work by the 'King' with one of the engine's best climbs of Wellington bank with 45mph maximum at Whiteball tunnel. The train ran pretty much on time or early all day, the engine achieving a respectable 51mph at the summit of Whiteball on the return.

19 May 2001

Minehead (WSR) to Swindon via Bristol TM; 13 coaches; 88 miles; fine, hot

While working on the West Somerset Railway the right-hand axle-box of the crank-axle (leading driving-wheel) had run hot. With this rail-tour scheduled, the locomotive was taken by road to Tyseley Locomotive Works for urgent repairs. This involved dismantling all the motion and dropping

the crank-axle out of the frames, repairing the axle box and then reassembling the whole thing. The cause of this failure was the disintegration of the worsted lubrication pad which presses against the journal. Without adjusting any of the spring positions, reweighing was considered unnecessary and the locomotive was returned to the WSR by road just in time.

After some good and uneventful work on the line from Minehead and then on from Taunton, the train arrived at Bristol on time and was joined by GW 'Castle' class No 5029 *Nunney Castle*, to continue to Paddington double-headed. Very soon after the departure from Bristol blue smoke was detected streaming from the left-hand middle driving-wheel axle-box. At Swindon the locomotive was removed from the train and delivered back to Tyseley by road. It appeared that a very slight rebalance had taken place as the locomotive was off-loaded at the WSR before the run and although stable while working unassisted, the alteration in the balance when double-headed brought additional weight onto this axle-box. The train proceeded to Paddington with No 5029 unassisted and made an on-time arrival.

12 May 2001 — Leaving Crowcombe on a West Somerset Railway service train to Bishop's Lydeard. *Richard Jones*

31 March 2002 — Easing through Smethwick Galton Bridge station where steam is a rarity, on a day of two runs between Birmingham Snow Hill and Worcester. *John Whitehouse*

9 September 2001

Tyseley to Stratford Upon Avon and return; nine coaches; 49 miles; not recorded

This was a loaded test train to check the repaired axle-box, which failed again.

After the much-improved performances by the 'King' during 2001 following the repair-work at Yeovil, the first hot-box came out of the blue and was an unwelcome set-back. Being particularly sensitive to precise weight-distribution and balancing because of its overall weight, it inevitably took the 'King' some time and a couple of trials to get things right again and finally prove the repairs. However, 2002 would see the complete rehabilitation of the locomotive and although the year was cut short the engine repeatedly made a name for itself in the best way possible.

2002

3 February 2002

Birmingham SH to Stratford-upon-Avon and return; nine coaches; 52 miles; cold, fine

This was the first loaded train hauled by No 6024 after its axle-box repairs. In December 2001, partnered by Tyseley's '94XX' Pannier No 9400, the locomotive had made a cautious excursion to Bescot and back

to see how things went. The next stage in the engine's rehabilitation was to build up some miles on the main line and the North Warwicks line was ideal for a morning run to Stratford and back with the support coach. After satisfactorily returning to Tyseley, this afternoon working was a proper trial of the locomotive and happily it came through without any problems.

31 March 2002

Birmingham SH to Worcester and return x two; nine coaches and nine coaches + Class 37; 134 miles; fine

This pair of runs in the same day left no doubts at all that the 'King' was back! The engine performed brightly all day and demonstrated free, rapid acceleration and fast running where the road allowed and some exceptional bursts of power when climbing Old Hill bank, creating a preservation record in the process. Draw-bar horse-power outputs on the first run were calculated well in excess of 1,950 on the bank, slightly less on the second run.

7 April 2002

Birmingham to Stratford-upon-Avon and return x two; nine coaches; 52 miles; cold, fine

Though without the excitement of the previous week's exploits because of the tender-first working and numerous speed restrictions, this next pair of runs saw further evidence that the 'King' was as sound and reliable as it had been before the spate of hot-boxes and it accumulated more useful miles on the clock. The first return from Stratford was taken gently throughout but the second run developed greater effort with the engine galloping along smoothly and culminated in a fierce piece of acceleration shortly before Tyseley.

13 April 2002 *(Table 16)*

Birmingham SH to Paddington via Oxford, and return; nine coaches; 260 miles; fine

With over 350 miles of loaded test trains and running-in completed, it was agreed that the 'King' had fully returned to health and was ready to resume its programme of long-distance main-line rail-tours. This tour, for Vintage Trains, proved to be an excellent run for the locomotive and an enjoyable excursion for those who travelled, culminating in an exceptional period of powerful climbing on Hatton bank.

The 'King' displayed some excellent work on the outbound run, particularly the dash to Hatton and the climb to Fosse Road, which kept a tight schedule under control. After Banbury, repeated signals at caution announced that our progress was tangled up with service trains and this continued virtually all the way to Paddington. The return was also a mixture of fluency and frustration. Driver Brian Ashford stated his intentions early as he seemed to have the devil after him; whenever the opportunity presented itself between adverse signals, he pressed the locomotive to good speeds but without apparent fuss.

BIRMINGHAM SNOW HILL to LONDON PADDINGTON
via OXFORD and return

Load: 9 coaches - 311 tons tare, 340 tons gross
Crew: *Drivers* R Poole (to London), B Ashford (to Birmingham)
Firemen A Llewelyn (to London), C Bayliss (to Birmingham)
Traction Inspectors G Jones (to London), R Hart (to Birmingham)
Weather: Cold, mainly fine but rain in the late morning

Distance		Schedule	Actual	Speeds
Miles/Ch.	BIRMINGHAM SNOW HILL	0	0.00	*start*
3.31	TYSELEY	12	7.29	*stop*
3.60	SOLIHULL	5	7.03	*stop*
3.30	DORRIDGE	4	5.35	*stop*
2.44	Lapworth	--	3.38	67
6.61	Hatton	9	7.24	67
12.68	Leamington Spa	17	17.21	23
23.79	*Fenny Compton*	29	29.1	65
32.59	BANBURY	43	38.51	*stop*
5.14	*Aynho Jn.*	7	8.45	41
10.75	Heyford	17	15.12	66
19.64	*Wolvercote Jn.*	26	26.58	44
22.55	Oxford	31	32.52	14
23.16	OXFORD UP & DOWN LOOP	33	34.41	*stop*
10.05	*Didcot East Jn.*	18	16.17	22 sigs
18.11	Goring & Streatley	--	27.38	43
26.73	Reading	47	46.34	19
38.52	Maidenhead	61	61.09	54
44.35	Slough	73	71.49	25
57.15	Ealing Broadway	--	86.35	34
60.78	Ladbroke Grove	95	94.22	43
62.68	PADDINGTON	100	100.17	*stop*
0.00	PADDINGTON	0	0.00	*start*
1.68	Ladbroke Grove	5	4.34	45
9.01	Southall	15	15.15	47
24.14	Maidenhead	36	34.32	72
35.73	Reading	49	50.02 *sigs*	*stop*
44.55	Goring & Streatley	--	61.26	72
53.05	Didcot Parkway	78	81.06	14 sigs
63.09	OXFORD UP & DOWN LOOP	104	104.01	*stop*
12.07	Heyford	18	20.01	67
23.02	BANBURY	32	40.46	*stop*
4.04	*Cropredy*	--	6.29	60
8.60	*Fenny Compton*	11	10.43	74
14.36	*Harbury Tunnel (N)*	--	15.21	73
19.71	Leamington Spa	22	20.45	35
21.64	Warwick	--	23.06	59
22.64	*MP 109*	--	24.05	64
23.64	*MP 110*	--	25.03	61
24.64	*MP 111*	--	26.03	59
25.78	Hatton	30	27.14	66
28.64	*MP 115*	--	29.39	77
32.59	DORRIDGE	38	34.25	*stop*
3.30	SOLIHULL	8	6.54	*stop*
3.60	TYSELEY	8	7.59	*stop*
3.31	BIRMINGHAM SNOW HILL	10	7.21	*stop*

Table 16: 13 April 2002

13 April 2002 — Successive generations of Western motive power at Old Oak Common. *Richard Jones*

After numerous frustrating checks, which lost a little time, the line cleared after Banbury and the locomotive flew up the climb past Cropredy, reaching a maximum of 65mph at the summit. The run onto Leamington was rapid to say the least and in no time at all, the engine was blasting away on the foothills of Hatton bank. Normally speed on Hatton bank is decayed slowly but surely, but not this time. Meeting the 1 in 114 at 58mph, speed was increased briefly to 64mph, before settling at a minimum of 59mph for the four and a half miles, achieving sustained average power outputs of over 1,800edbhp for three and a half miles. Observers concluded that this was the fastest climb of Hatton bank in preservation with this load; more importantly it was confirmation that the 'King' was entirely restored to full fitness.

27 July 2002
Didcot to Taunton and the West Somerset Railway, via Reading and Westbury; 10 coaches; 123 miles; fine
Following the Birmingham-Paddington run the locomotive spent almost three months on the Watercress Line (Mid-Hants Railway) where it put in a number of exciting climbs of the 'Alps'. It then made this run to the West Somerset Railway to position for another visit to South Devon. The run was faultless in every respect and no time was lost by the locomotive.

EXETER to PAR and return

Load: 9 coaches - 314 tons tare, 350 tons gross
Crew: *Drivers* C Hopcroft (to Par), G Ewans (to Plymouth), P Burns (to Exeter)
Firemen F Lewis (to Par), P Burns (to Plymouth), G Ewans (to Exeter)
Traction Inspectors A Fenn (to Par), R Moss (To Exeter)
Weather: Fine, dry, sunny

Distance		Schedule	Actual	Speeds
Miles/Ch.	EXETER St. DAVIDS	0	0.00	*start*
4.67	*Starcross*	--	10.40	68
10.42	Dawlish Warren	13	12.24	68
20.14	Newton Abbot	26	21.24	52
21.08	*MP 215 (Aller Jn.)*	--	22.32	49/55
23.71	*Dainton tunnel (East)*	--	25.58	33
28.74	Totnes	43	31.40	56
33.48	*MP 227/II Rattery*	--	38.09	45/50
38.08	*MP 232 Wrangaton*	--	43.39	54/58
40.35	Ivybridge	61	46.07	57
52.04	PLYMOUTH NORTH ROAD	80	65.31	*stop*
1.20	Devonport	--	3.40	31
2.72	*St Budeaux Ferry Road*	16	10.19	11
4.20	Saltash	--	14.59	16
9.21	St Germans	--	22.50	19
14.53	Menheniot	--	31.52	56
17.63	Liskeard	41	35.38	45
21.05	Doublebois	--	40.02	36
22.73	*MP 270 Largin*	--	43.21	34
26.75	Bodmin Parkway	--	48.20	49/55
30.28	Lostwithiel	61	52.55	32
34.58	PAR	80	64.16	*stop*
0.00	PAR	0	0.00	*start*
4.30	Lostwithiel	17	18.34	17
7.63	Bodmin Parkway	--	26.03	23
11.65	*MP 270 Largin*	--	45.18	17 *slip*
16.75	Liskeard	29	54.02	16/29
25.37	St Germans	--	66.05	47
30.38	Saltash	49	72.34	24
31.51	*St Budeaux Ferry Road*	--	75.43	41
34.58	PLYMOUTH NORTH ROAD	65	82.03	*stop*
2.08	*Laira Jn.*	--	4.44	67
3.76	*MP 242*	--	6.30	62
6.66	*Hemerdon*	--	10.52	38
11.49	Ivybridge	19	16.24	51
13.76	*MP 232 Wrangaton*	--	19.07	52
16.16	*Brent*	--	21.22	60
23.10	Totnes	33	28.31	60
28.13	*Dainton tunnel (East)*	--	34.03	43
30.67	*MP 215 (Aller Jn.)*	--	36.48	54
31.71	Newton Abbot	45	37.56	65
37.03	Teignmouth	--	42.33	57
41.42	Dawlish Warren	60	46.58	63
45.26	*Powderham Crossing*	--	50.06	77
50.44	*City Basin Jn.*	--	54.21	74
52.04	EXETER St. DAVIDS	72	58.06	*stop*

31 August 2002 *(Table 17)*

Exeter to Par via Plymouth and return; nine coaches; 173 miles; fine

There was no reason to suspect that this day would bring anything *extra*-special. The locomotive's recent form had been on a par with the best it had ever achieved but most people assumed that it had already produced all it could on the Plymouth road. After all, on two of the four key climbing sections, the locomotive already held the records for the fastest times, as well as being the quickest between Aller Junction and Plympton. But by the end of the day, with the bar raised by a couple of steps at least, it was generally accepted that the run was as good as anything seen in preservation, by any locomotive.

The fine weather in which the early-morning light-engine move from Taunton was made lifted the spirits and Driver Chris Hopcroft and his mate Fred Lewis seemed to catch this mood. Leaving Exeter 10.5min down with a sold-out train appeared to be just the incentive for some fine work. After a silky glide along the seawall, rather than approach the first climb as fast as possible to achieve about 60mph at the foot of Dainton, this time the engine's approach was at 49mph but accelerating, so that at the beginning of the bank speed was being gained rather than lost. The 'King' continued to storm up the bank and with only a mile to go its speed was still 51mph. On a tight curve approaching the tunnel a flange-greaser caught Chris out and a sudden if brief slip took the edge off the locomotive's progress. Even so, it entered the tunnel at 33mph and still managed to match its previously fastest time for the climb (achieved on 19 September 1998).

The train tore on down to Totnes at line speed and thundered its way onto Rattery bank (where No 6024 already held the record, also since September 1999). Without the hint of any loss of adhesion, the locomotive motored on, it seemed with unlimited energy, eating up the gradient and, once over the steepest part, there was no question of a let-up; speed rapidly increased to the line-speed and a new time on Rattery 10sec better than the best had been set. This progress continued right down to Plympton where signals reduced the early arrival at Plymouth to nearly four minutes but a net gain of over 14min on the schedule. Chris and Fred left the footplate at Plymouth to well-deserved plaudits and were replaced by the Bristol Barton Hill duo of Paul Burns and Geoff Ewans, who, after watering, took the train onto Par. Despite a late departure from Plymouth and a tough route, the running was carried out with ease and the arrival at Par was over five minutes early.

The return to Plymouth was marred by signal stops early on and a bout of slipping due to more rail-greasers on the climb to Doublebois, which forced a 25min late arrival at North Road. Brisk watering reduced the deficit to a 12min late departure from Plymouth, which left one hour exactly for the 52 miles to Exeter. Although theoretically feasible, achieving a right-time arrival at Exeter in 60min would require a high level of quality driving and firing, a fully-responsive locomotive and considerable benevolence from Control. In the event all three were delivered in maximum quantities and with each rapidly succeeding minute, another sensational chapter in the dramatic story of No 6024 unfolded in front of the breathless passengers.

Climbing as strongly as a 'King' can and running downhill as fast as the line allowed, not a single second was wasted and the driver and fireman never put a foot wrong. After all the hard work to Aller Junction, there was always the risk a Paignton service train would be put out ahead, but unusually this was avoided and with seven minutes saved up to Newton Abbot, the 60min target was still possible. Sweeping beside the Teign estuary and along the seawall the dreaded brake application, which would once and for all put a stop to this matchless progress, just didn't happen. Instead, curving around the corner through Dawlish Warren with speed increasing to the day's maximum of 78mph at Powderham Crossing, a clear approach to Exeter was signalled and a two-minute early arrival produced another record — a staggering 58min 6sec from the start at Plymouth.

6 October 2002 *(Table 18)*

Birmingham SH to Paddington via High Wycombe and return via Oxford; nine coaches + Class 47; 241 miles; fine

As a part of the 150th anniversary celebrations of Snow Hill station, this run took place with a set of Pullmans (plus a Class 47 providing power for train air-conditioning). Unfortunately, the bulk of the stock had fixed windows so most people missed the music from the locomotive. The train was a substantial load of 465 tons. After an on-time departure from Snow Hill and passing *Rood Ashton Hall* heading towards Birmingham, the train made its way southwards, stopping at Dorridge which was hosting its own celebrations and where a huge crowd had assembled. With a very tight schedule through the outskirts it was impossible to keep to time but, beyond Dorridge, some sustained work was possible and stirring progress was made to Banbury.

A delay leaving Banbury was extended beyond Aynho, with an irritating sequence of temporary speed restrictions on the newly-doubled Chiltern Line and, apart from a handful of episodes when the locomotive could be given its head, the restrictions continued almost into London and the delay gradually grew. Arrival in Paddington was 36min late. Departure from Paddington for the return was on-time and good progress punctuated by signals and gauging checks was made along the Great Western main line to Didcot. Lively running either side of the water stop at Oxford kept people interested and, following another delay for pathing at Banbury, a measured climb through Cropredy was followed by some real fun which took place on Hatton bank again. This time there would be no question of beating the speeds attained on April's run, especially as the train was held at signals at Leamington Spa station, but the effort produced by the locomotive on the climb was simply astonishing. With speeds fixed in the low-50s for the entire

26 October 2002 — Accelerating westwards down from Whiteball summit on a Birmingham to Kingswear and return charter. *Dave Richards*

BIRMINGHAM SNOW HILL to LONDON PADDINGTON via H WYCOMBE, return via OXFORD

Load: 9 coaches (+ Class 47 for Air Con) - 442 tons tare, 464 tons gross
Crew: *Drivers* R Churchill (to Banbury, from Reading), B Dudley-Ward (to Reading)
          Firemen D Morris (to Reading), A Meanley (to Birmingham)
          Traction Inspectors R Churchill, B Dudley-Ward
Weather: Dry, sunny, warming up throughout

Distance		Schedule	Actual	Speeds
Miles/Ch.	BIRMINGHAM SNOW HILL	0	0.00	start
3.31	TYSELEY	9	9.35	stop
3.60	SOLIHULL	5	8.12	stop
3.30	DORRIDGE	5	6.40	stop
2.44	Lapworth	--	4.16	62
6.61	Hatton	9	7.57	70
12.68	Leamington Spa	17	14.04	35
23.79	*Fenny Compton*	29	25.14	68
32.59	BANBURY UG LOOP	39	35.52	stop
5.14	*Aynho Jn.*	6	9.04	20 check
14.16	Bicester N.	16	25.07	22 check
27.07	Haddenham	26	44.09	54 check
32.72	Princes Risborough	34	52.28	40
36.05	Saunderton	--	56.33	43
41.03	High Wycombe	44	63.14	40
45.71	Beaconsfield	50	68.48	38
52.62	Denham	--	78.00	33 check
55.44	West Ruislip	--	82.47	34 check
57.25	South Ruislip	65	86.00	29 check
64.27	*Old Oak Common W. Jn.*	81	101.54	35
65.54	Ladbroke Grove	--	103.48 *sigs*	42
67.42	PADDINGTON	89	109.35	stop
0.00	PADDINGTON	0	0.00	start
9.01	Southall	18	14.20	27 check
24.14	Maidenhead	39	33.11	62
35.73	Reading	57	49.53 *sigs*	24
44.55	Goring & Streatley	--	60.12	68
53.05	Didcot North Jn.	77	83.03	28
63.09	OXFORD UP & DOWN LOOP	90	98.47	stop
12.07	Heyford	18	19.30	71
17.68	Aynho Jn.	27	26.59 *sigs*	20
23.02	BANBURY	32	42.48	stop pathing
4.04	*Cropredy*	--	10.02	43
8.60	*Fenny Compton*	14	15.18	65
14.36	*Harbury Tunnel (N)*	--	20.25	61
19.71	LEAMINGTON SPA	26	27.26 *sigs*	stop pathing
1.73	Warwick	--	5.01	41
3.73	*MP110*	--	7.23	53
4.73	*MP111*	--	8.32	54
5.73	*MP112*	--	9.39	54
6.07	Hatton	8	9.51	56
8.73	*MP 115*	--	12.37	64
55.61	DORRIDGE	15	17.41	stop
3.30	SOLIHULL	5	6.58	stop
3.60	TYSELEY	5	8.34	stop
3.31	BIRMINGHAM SNOW HILL	10	8.01	stop

climb, it was calculated that the locomotive broke the magic 2,000 mark for draw-bar horsepower continuously between Warwick and the summit, with an outright maximum of 2,120. The fireworks continued all the way to Snow Hill where the arrival was an inconsequential four minutes late.

26 October 2002 *(Table 19)*

Birmingham SH to Kingswear via Worcester, Bristol TM and Paignton and return to Worcester; 10 coaches; 374 miles; cold, mainly dry, with rain later

This marathon appeared to be compromised from the word go, first by some unhelpful station work at Snow Hill and Control. The late departure was extended by a series of checks and poor hydrant pressure at Worcester Shrub Hill. In between times the 'King' showed all the energy it had exhibited in recent months and this continued with some fine speedy work before Cheltenham and Barnwood Junction. Beyond Standish Junction came the liveliest running of the day, with over 78mph on Stonehouse Viaduct and a superb climb to Rangeworthy after Wickwar tunnel which was entered at over 72mph, enabling some of the lateness to be clawed back. Thereafter the performance badly fell away, with a clinkered fire hampering steaming all the way to Taunton. A conservative climb was made up Wellington bank and this appeared to revive the fire because after Tiverton, through Exeter, along the seawall, on the undulating branch to Paignton and onto Kingswear, the fire appeared to be behaving itself, with sparkling work by the engine.

The 203-mile outbound leg having consumed a good part of the morning's tender of coal, it was necessary to reload almost completely from the P&DSR's supply of coal. After returning to Kingswear, the loco immediately appeared to be in trouble, with a laboured climb through Torquay leading to bad slipping and eventually coming to a full stand on Torre bank. After a couple of attempts with yet more slipping, a restart was successfully achieved, but it was clear that all was far from well in the firebox, with poor steaming and yet more weary running along the flat towards Dawlish. The train eventually crawled into Exeter, 46min down.

Attempts to clean the fire and get an even chance of proceeding were thwarted by the quality of the coal, which simply would not burn with any heat and rapidly turned to clinker. A blow-up before Tiverton Junction and more efforts to rally the fire in Tiverton loop further delayed the run and eventually the run with steam was effectively *hors de combat* at Taunton, where diesel traction took over the train. This was a sad end to what had promised to be an exceptional day for the passengers. The diesel piloted the train as far as Worcester where the train was terminated and passengers motored to their destinations. Later in the week the loco and coach returned to Tyseley. Routine examination revealed that the thickness of the tyres on the rear driving wheels had reached their permitted limit and needed replacing before the engine could run again.

The abrupt end of No 6024's second main-line ticket came as a surprise and was not the ideal way the engine would have gone out. However, as far as the driving wheel tyres were concerned, they had been living on borrowed time for years and it was considered a better option to bring the entire overhaul forward rather than take the engine out of traffic, await delivery of the new tyres and then return to traffic for just a handful of months. It took a few weeks to prepare the overhaul facilities at Tyseley Locomotive Works and tie up all the funding but by January 2003 work started on dismantling the engine.

As before the process went efficiently, using a combination of the Society's volunteers and contractors and no horrors were discovered. Apart from completely repiping the air-braking, replacing the ash-pan (with hopper doors underneath) and fitting Train Protection Warning System (TPWS) the locomotive was left well-alone. Well into the reassembly phase a cracked super-heater header caused a hiatus in progress, but in early October 2004, less than two years after its final main-line run, and after 21 months work, No 6024 entered the fray once again.

This time the Society decided that the locomotive would be available for hire only after it had been thoroughly proved in main-line trials building up a considerable mileage. Therefore, a programme was devised similar to the work done by locomotives out-shopped from Swindon Works in steam days, first taking No 6024 and its support coach on a morning trip to Bescot and if all went well an afternoon run to Stratford-upon-Avon. As paths on the North Warwicks line were unavailable, this run and the subsequent programme of evening trains all used the main line to Hatton.

2004

19 to 22 October 2004
Acocks Green to Stratford-upon-Avon and return to Birmingham SH x four; eight coaches; 52 miles
These trains were the next phase of the locomotive's trials. Running tender-first to Stratford prevented any high speeds on the outbound and unfortunately each of the first three inbound were frustrated by signals so there could be no real test at speed. However, on the fourth and final run the locomotive was able to stretch its legs on the return, demonstrating rapid acceleration and brief glimpses of its permitted top speed. With almost 300 miles without anything amiss the future augured well.

26 October 2004
Worcester to Ealing Broadway via Oxford; 10 coaches; 114 miles; fine
This was the Society's own rail-tour, the final part of the trials' programme to prove the engine and reintroduce it to main-line traffic. The route moved the locomotive to London for next programme. What a run! The evenings during the previous week had not only tested the locomotive but had freed it up and this was used to great effect throughout the day. The aggressive climb of Campden bank produced a minimum of 50mph with a considerable margin in hand. Rapid progress continued, touching

BIRMINGHAM SNOW HILL to KINGSWEAR

Load: 10 Coaches - 348 tons tare, 375 tons gross
Crew: *Drivers* C Bayliss (to Bristol), G Ewans (to Paignton), P&DSR (to Kingswear)
Firemen R Poole (to Bristol), P Burns (to Paignton), P&DSR (to Kingswear)
Traction Inspector G Jones (to Paignton)
Weather: Dry, cold, strong prevailing wind

Distance		Schedule	Actual	Speeds
Miles/Ch.	BIRMINGHAM SNOW HILL	0	0.00	*start*
7.00	*Old Hill tunnel (east)*	--	15.58	24/27
7.41	*Old Hill tunnel (west)*	--	17.13	18
9.30	Cradley Heath	--	20.09	33
12.01	STOURBRIDGE JN.	24	26.14	*stop*
3.42	Blakedown	--	5.15	70
6.50	Kidderminster	9	8.16	62
16.06	DROITWICH SPA	20	20.31	*stop*
5.48	WORCESTER SHRUB HILL	10	10.20	*stop*
14.54	Ashchurch	30	18.22	74
21.76	CHELTENHAM SPA	39	25.51	*stop*
12.41	*Standish Jn.*	17	16.18	64
18.04	Cam & Dursley	--	20.47	77
28.00	*Wickwar tunnel (north)*	--	28.49	73
33.58	*Westerleigh Jn. (pathing stop)*	40	35.36	*stop*
4.70	BRISTOL PARKWAY	12	14.48	*stop*
4.19	STAPLETON ROAD	10	10.59	*stop*
1.48	Bristol Temple Meads	7	7.16	12
3.32	Parson Street	--	13.09	40
9.50	Nailsea and Backwell	--	20.23	66
13.45	Yatton	--	23.56	60
18.28	*Worle Jn.*	26	30.01	50
21.21	*Uphill Jn.*	28	33.26	52
28.42	Highbridge	34	42.11	49
34.64	Bridgwater	40	50.08	50
41.67	*Cogload Jn.*	47	59.20	46
46.19	TAUNTON	54	66.58	*stop*
0.00	TAUNTON	0	0.00	*start*
4.33	*Bradford Crossing*	--	11.47	51
7.07	*Wellington*	--	14.58	51
10.01	*Whiteball tunnel (East)*	--	19.02	34
10.68	*MP 174 Whiteball Summit*	--	20.47	29
14.16	Tiverton Parkway	22	24.35	46
15.78	TIVERTON DOWN LOOP	29	29.25	*stop*
6.31	*Hele & Bradninch*	--	7.51	75
11.06	*Stoke Canon*	--	11.35	75
15.56	Exeter St. Davids	24	16.54	26
16.22	*City Basin Jn.*	--	19.18	52
21.40	*Powderham Crossing*	--	24.11	68
25.24	DAWLISH WARREN	41	31.13	*stop*
4.39	Teignmouth	--	6.59	59
9.51	Newton Abbot	15	12.29	41
10.55	*MP 215 Aller Jn.*	--	14.18	37
15.45	Torquay	--	21.44	31
17.58	PAIGNTON	31	26.51	*stop*
6.52	KINGSWEAR	26	17.41	*stop*

4 October 2004 — Fresh from the Works after its 2002-04 overhaul, a trial steaming and Press Day at Tyseley before a series of test runs. *Mike Wild/Steam Railway*

84mph at Kingham. A couple of TPWS brake applications occurred while the crew got accustomed to the system.

After a crew change, further good progress was made along the Great Western mail line Up Relief but unfortunately the train passed a red signal at Pangbourne and the driver was subsequently suspended. This rather clouded what had been a very successful first long-distance outing for the 'King' but the free-running strength the engine had demonstrated, with copious steam available and no mechanical problems was extremely encouraging.

13 November 2004

Bristol TM to Plymouth and return; nine coaches; 251 miles; fine
The locomotive was called up as substitute for No 71000 *Duke of Gloucester* (which was scheduled to make its first visit to South Devon). After a decent climb of Wellington bank, the crew had a good stab at the tricky territory in South Devon and despite the standing start from Newton Abbot, the engine was well in control on Dainton. It also found Rattery to its liking, making the climb over the measured distance in 6min 25sec, second only to No 6024's run in August 2002. Arrival in Plymouth was 11min early.

The climb of Hemerdon, solid at first, was jeopardised first by one slip, then another and although there was little danger of a stall, speed rapidly

<table>
<tr><td colspan="4">BRISTOL TEMPLE MEADS to PLYMOUTH, return to EXETER</td></tr>
<tr><td>Load:</td><td colspan="3">9 coaches - 333 tons tare, 358 tons gross</td></tr>
<tr><td>Crew:</td><td colspan="3">Drivers T Rees (to Newton Abbot), G Ewans (to Plymouth), P Burns (to Exeter)</td></tr>
<tr><td></td><td colspan="3">Firemen F Lewis (to Newton Abbot), P Burns (to Plymouth), G Ewans (to Exeter)</td></tr>
<tr><td></td><td colspan="3">Traction Inspectors R Moss (to Newton Abbot, C Rooker (to Exeter)</td></tr>
<tr><td>Weather:</td><td colspan="3">Fine, dry, cold</td></tr>
</table>

Distance		Schedule	Actual	Speeds
Miles/Ch.	BRISTOL TEMPLE MEADS	0	0.00	*start*
8.02	Nailsea and Backwell	--	10.12	77
11.77	Yatton	--	13.17	78
16.60	*Worle Jn.*	22	17.52	66
19.53	*Uphill Jn.*	24.30	20.21	74
26.74	Highbridge	30.30	26.09	76
33.16	Bridgwater	36.30	31.38	70
40.19	*Cogload Jn.*	44	37.25	75
<u>44.61</u>	TAUNTON	<u>50</u>	<u>42.52</u>	*stop*
4.33	*Bradford Crossing*	--	6.17	63
7.07	*Wellington*	--	8.42	65
10.01	*Whiteball tunnel (East)*	--	11.45	49
10.68	*MP 174 Whiteball Summit*	--	12.49	46
14.16	Tiverton Parkway	20.30	15.54	68
<u>15.78</u>	TIVERTON DOWN LOOP	<u>23</u>	<u>20.00</u>	*stop*
6.31	*Hele & Bradninch*	--	8.08	71
11.06	*Stoke Canon*	--	12.23	65
15.56	Exeter St. Davids	19.30	16.30	27
16.22	*City Basin Jn.*	--	18.40	56
21.40	*Powderham Crossing*	--	23.19	70
25.24	Dawlish Warren	36	26.41	64
<u>34.75</u>	NEWTON ABBOT	<u>51</u>	<u>51.00</u>	*stop*
1.09	*MP 215 (Aller Jn.)*	--	3.29	25
3.73	*Dainton tunnel (East)*	--	7.51	31
8.67	Totnes	17	14.17 *sigs*	45
9.15	*MP 223/I*	--	*stops*	--
13.27	*MP 227/III Rattery*	--	31.29	34
17.76	*MP 232 Wrangaton*	--	38.01	46
21.05	Ivybridge	34	40.37	58
25.04	Hemerdon	40	45.31	58
<u>29.69</u>	PLYMOUTH NORTH ROAD	<u>53</u>	<u>54.39</u>	*stop*
0.00	PLYMOUTH NORTH ROAD	0	0.00	*start*
3.76	*MP 242*	--	7.03	61
6.66	*Hemerdon*	16	12.28	35
11.49	Ivybridge	--	18.44	44
13.76	*MP 232 Wrangaton*	--	22.00	44
16.16	*Brent*	--	24.32	56
23.10	Totnes	35	32.14	60
28.13	*Dainton tunnel (East)*	--	38.46	30
30.67	*MP 215 (Aller Jn.)*	--	41.49	55
31.71	Newton Abbot	50	42.54	59
37.03	Teignmouth	--	47.56	56
41.42	Dawlish Warren	61	56.10 *sigs*	18
45.26	*Powderham Crossing*	--	62.24	63
50.44	*City Basin Jn.*	--	67.33 *sigs*	29
<u>52.04</u>	EXETER St. DAVIDS	<u>74</u>	<u>73.03</u>	*stop*

Table 20: 29 January 2005

fell off, demonstrating vividly how tricky this climb can be. With only the short side of Dainton to come the engine and crew had reason to be satisfied with the day's work which ended back in Bristol with some very happy passengers.

11 December 2004

Bristol TM to Paddington and return; 11/10 coaches; 237 miles; cold, fine
The 50min schedule for the 40 miles from Bristol Temple Meads to Swindon was on the tight side and, despite some strong work throughout, a couple of checks lost more time after a late departure. Time was recovered at the water-stop and with speeds in the high 60s to Didcot all the delay had been made up. More good progress was maintained to Slough but a few minutes were dropped before Paddington. Against a much easier schedule time-keeping was much better and, after touching 84mph down Dauntsey bank, arrival at Temple Meads was seven minutes early. This was a very competent performance by the engine.

30 December 2004

Victoria to Stratford Upon Avon via High Wycombe and return to Paddington; 11 coaches; 243 miles; cold, dry, overcast
With an unfriendly schedule on a number of sections, plus a plethora of checks, the performance, however good, would be unlikely to keep time on this run although some efficient work at the water-stops enabled recovery along the way so the timings were never seriously out of control. This was another solid, reliable show by the locomotive, and the EWS crews from Dollands Moor, Hither Green, Saltley, Didcot and Hoo Junction all did their bit to provide a good day out.

2004 ended on a high note with the engine having performed immaculately for almost every mile it had worked since returning from overhaul. This pattern was to continue into 2005 as No 6024 embarked on an intensive programme of varied work involving many of its familiar routes.

2005

29 January 2005 *(Table 20)*

Bristol TM to Plymouth and return; nine coaches; 251 miles; fine
Another return to South Devon provided further insight into the genuine challenges presented by this line and how the 'King' copes. A 15min late departure from Bristol was reduced to eight minutes late for the pathing stop at Taunton after the locomotive was pressed very hard by the Newport crew. The climb of the lower slopes of Wellington was vigorous

BIRMINGHAM to NEWPORT and return via BROMSGROVE and GLOUCESTER

Load:	9 coaches - 313 tons tare, 340 tons gross
Crew:	*Driver/Inspector* R Churchill
	Firemen Dean Morris (to Newport), Alastair Meanley (to Birmingham)
Weather:	Overcast, cold, some sunshine diminishing to drizzle

Distance		Schedule	Actual	Speeds
Miles/Ch.	St.ANDREWS Jn (Sig.SY92)	0	0.00	*start*
5.52	Kings Norton	21	23.34	13
10.60	Barnt Green	29	33.17	51
14.23	Bromsgrove	35	36.57	72
16.36	Stoke Works Jn.	37	38.43	77
27.53	Abbotswood Jn.	47	47.32	74
36.10	Bredon	--	54.43	78
39.21	Ashchurch	57	56.37	18 *check*
41.59	Cleeve	--	61.05	69
45.43	Cheltenham Spa	67	65.07	17 *check*
51.06	Barnwood Crossing	73	73.02 *sigs*	*stop*
52.03	GLOUCESTER	78	82.56	*stop*
11.04	Newnham Tunnel	--	14.22	61
14.18	Awre Crossing	16	17.14	68
19.33	Lydney	20	22.14	63
27.29	Chepstow	30	29.53	36 *check*
31.76	Portskewett	--	34.36	74
34.57	Severn Tunnel Jn.	39	40.21	20
44.46	NEWPORT	62	57.56	*stop*
0.00	NEWPORT	0	0.00	*start*
9.69	Severn Tunnel Jn.	27	22.22	19
12.50	Portskewett	--	28.01	34
17.17	Chepstow	42	35.04	28
25.13	Lydney	52	43.46	62
30.28	Awre Crossing	57	48.40	64
33.31	Newnham Tunnel	--	51.30	67
44.46	GLOUCESTER	72	63.16	*stop*
0.77	Barnwood Jn.	4	3.45	30
6.40	Cheltenham Spa	10	10.19	41
10.24	Cleeve	--	16.02	63
13.62	Ashchurch	18	19.47	35 *check*
15.73	Bredon	--	22.23	62
24.38	Abbotswood Jn.	28	29.13	74
35.55	Stoke Works Jn.	39	39.59	25
37.48	BROMSGROVE	44	46.06	*stop*
0.50	MP 55	--	2.20	25
1.10	MP 54/II	--	3.24	29
2.10	MP 53/II	--	5.23	30
3.10	MP 52/II	--	7.04	37
3.63	Barnt Green	12	8.07	40
8.71	Kings Norton	21	14.55	28
14.43	St.ANDREWS Jn (Sig.SY92)	36	33.03	*stop*

drawbar horsepower of 1,900 — almost 100% of its maximum potential — for a brief period, without any slipping.

As an early pass of Totnes was now likely there was the risk we would catch up the service train ahead and so it proved as yellow signals indicated that the unit was still on Rattery. The train drifted slowly through Totnes over three minutes early and with speeds dropping to single figures, onto the 1 in 66 at the foot of the bank. Opened up to keep momentum, the locomotive slipped badly and briefly came to a stop between MPs 223 and 223/I. Starting again, then more slipping, another stop longer this time, then slowly easing forward and this time the engine kept its feet. Another slip on the 1 in 46/52 just before Tigley and a couple more afterwards lost some momentum but once onto the 1 in 90 the worst of the climb had been dealt with. Overcoming this challenge was the clearest evidence of the suitability of this engine for these climbs, demonstrating to good effect exactly what they were built for.

With speeds still in the low 40s on the easier higher stretches the train was almost six minutes down by the summit but eventually the lateness into Plymouth was only four minutes. There were no dramas and no records on the return run and an early pass along the seawall was halted by signals at Dawlish Warren, bringing an arrival in Exeter just a few seconds early.

26 February 2005 *(Table 21)*

Tyseley to Newport via Bromsgrove and Gloucester and return; nine coaches; 208 miles; fine, then wet.

This run featured some very high power outputs (including briefly touching the 2,000 drawbar horsepower mark) accompanied by fierce acceleration and very fast running on both the outbound and inward runs including over 81mph south of Abbotswood Junction, with 22 miles at an average of over 76mph. With various clearance checks and a very tight schedule all day, the crew fortunately never put a foot wrong. The climax of the day was the first haulage by the 'King' of a train up the two miles of the Lickey incline's 1 in 37, a job done in nasty drizzle with the prudent assistance — much to the disgust of some observers — of a Class 37 banker. As it would have been inconceivable that any locomotive would have been expected to take this load up unassisted in steam days it would have been irresponsible to try it now. With the 'King' making a finely-balanced ascent without any slipping the banker duly applied full power initially and gradually reduced its contribution towards the top of the bank.

28 February 2005

Taunton to Paignton and return; 12 VSOE coaches; 118 miles; fine

For almost a quarter of a century, more than anyone else, Bernard Staite has influenced and promoted preserved steam on the main line. This train, made up of the Venice Simplon Orient Express (VSOE) Pullmans was hauled by No 6024 heading the Severn Valley Railway's 'Manor' class No 7802 *Bradley Manor*, was run to celebrate a great career advancing main line steam and to mark Bernard's retirement. The day saw some lively running as the two locomotives had more than ample power to handle this

although the effort near the top fell away a little, suggesting diminishing boiler pressure. Water was taken on time at Tiverton and a rapid descent allowed an early pass of Exeter. At Newton Abbot the Barton Hill men took over for the rest of the day. Restarting immediately behind a service train denied the 'King' a good run at the bank but accelerating powerfully when it got beyond MP215, the locomotive was still going at over 30mph when it arrived at the tunnel. It had produced an average estimated

LONDON to WORCESTER via OXFORD

Load: 10 coaches - 337 tons tare, 360 tons gross
Crew: *Driver/Inspector P Kirk*
Fireman J Fletcher
Weather: Fine, dry, intermittant sunshine

Distance		Schedule	Actual	Speeds
Miles/Ch.	WILLESDEN SW Sidings	0	0.00	start
15.20	Slough	27.30	35.00	32
19.30	Taplow	--	40.07	60
21.00	MAIDENHEAD	35	42.54	stop
4.80	Twyford	9.30	10.05	20
11.70	READING	16	18.03	stop
5.45	Pangbourne	--	8.20	68
8.62	Goring & Streatley	--	11.01	75
12.39	Cholsey & Moulsford	--	13.54	78
17.12	DIDCOT	21	22.15	stop
5.30	Radley	--	8.16	67
8.00	Kennington Junction	17	10.34	74
10.00	OXFORD UP LOOP	21.30	15.43	stop
2.90	*Wolvercot Junction*	6	6.06	44
11.60	Finstock	--	15.02	69
13.20	Charlbury	--	16.28	68
16.90	Ascott-Under-Wychwood	26	20.01	55
28.30	Moreton-in-Marsh	42.30	34.52	stop
31.50	Blockley Crossing	--	41.03	73
33.50	Chipping Camden	--	42.46	70
35.50	*MP 99*	--	44.27	69
38.20	Honeybourne	--	46.50	77
43.30	EVESHAM SB	63	53.40	stop
5.80	Pershore	--	7.33	76
8.00	Stoulton	--	9.27	64
10.50	*Norton Jn.*	22.30	13.40	18
13.60	WORCESTER SHRUB HILL	28	20.42	stop

Table 22: 21 May 2005

19 March 2005 — Lining up at Minehead with No 4936 *Kinlet Hall*, No 7822 *Foxcote Manor* and No 5051 *Earl Bathurst*, during the West Somerset Railway's Spring Gala. *Terry Bennett*

21 May 2005 *(Table 22)*

Victoria to Worcester via Swindon and return; 11 coaches; 305 miles; fine
This was the first of four in the 'Cathedrals Express' programme by the engine. An interesting operation was complicated by the need to get from Old Oak Common to Victoria in the morning and back in the evening, further complicated by a ban on the 'King' entering the platform in Victoria in the evening because of gauging. The running was strong in the meantime, apart from on the return south of Worcester, where it appeared there was a temporary difficulty with the steaming. The climb of Sapperton was lively and taken with ease, culminating in a creditable 37mph at the tunnel.

4 June 2005

Victoria to Weymouth via Reading and Castle Cary; 11 coaches + Class 31; 162 miles; fine
This rail-tour should have taken the 'King' out as far as Yeovil (for servicing) and then back from Weymouth. This became a distant hope after a couple of hours. The Class 31 was there to drag the stock into Victoria and then to give the train a shove out; then, making its own way to Yeovil it would haul the train to Weymouth and then assist the 'King' on Upwey bank. Apparently its driver didn't sign the road planned for it so instead it stayed on the train all the way — the equivalent of three extra coaches. It transpired *en route* that the Class 31 was also suffering brake problems and repairs along the way caused an accumulation of delays which in the end became irretrievable.

In addition, doubts about the diesel's ability to haul the train up Evershot bank were eventually revealed and at Frome the 'King' was rerostered to take the train to Weymouth. The 'King' had performed impeccably for the entire run but with heavier than planned usage of coal and water. The additional mileage proved to be on the limit of the available coal in the tender.

heavy train and the only blemish was an air system failure on No 6024 at Paignton which required attention before the train could leave with the return working in the evening.

12 March 2005

Gloucester to Minehead (WSR) via Bristol TM and Taunton; 13 coaches + Class 50; 86 miles; fine
This enormous train located the 'King' at the WSR and was worked unassisted all the way to Minehead.

23 April 2005

Exeter to Par via Plymouth and return; 13 coaches; 173 miles; fine
Another double-headed effort with 'Castle' class No 5029 *Nunney Castle* returned No 6024 to South Devon again, with both engines putting in plenty of action. On the return from Plymouth, after the 20mph restriction at the arch bridge at Plympton for the cab-roof of the 'Castle', a fast run followed to Exeter and was not far outside the 60min mark.

14 August 2005 — The westbound 'Torbay Express' curves along the seawall to Teignmouth station on its way to Kingswear before servicing and returning to Bristol.
Dave Richards

18 June 2005
Victoria to Gloucester via Swindon and return; 11 coaches; 248 miles; fine, very hot
On the hottest day of the year so far the locomotive again gave a good account of itself, but experienced a bad bout of priming before Reading. A signal failure after Standish Junction of the return prevented a normal climb of Sapperton and the requirement to check with Control at each signal on the climb had everyone on their toes. A heavier load might have caused problems but as it was, by dint of some skilled, sensitive work by Driver Chris Hopcroft, apart from one brief slip the 'King' handled the crisis without problems.

2 July 2005 *(Table 23)*
Paddington to Kingswear via Reading and Frome, return to Taunton; 11 coaches; 290 miles; fine
To celebrate the engine's 75th Anniversary the Society held an event for its Members a week earlier at Old Oak Common. Then, the Society sponsored an ambitious rail-tour replicating a 'King'-hauled named train of GW days over a traditional 'King' route, to run almost to the day the locomotive had been put to work 75 years earlier.

An early start was necessary to ensure a path out of Paddington but this allowed use of the Down Main as far as Reading where the first stop was made after an early arrival. Just before an early restart a certain publisher made it onto the train by the skin of his teeth, sprinting along the platform to the last coach (he seemed to have recovered by mid-afternoon!). Still running early, the train continued to the first water-stop just beyond Newbury Racecourse and then on towards Savernake summit. Leaving Newbury, a slightly under-prepared fire inhibited anything too dramatic on the climb, but many felt that the unfussy running reminded them of how 'Kings' were used daily in steam days; we were four minutes down by the stop at Westbury. Much livelier work followed the re-start from Frome and a strong climb of Brewham bank was followed by the train sweeping swiftly over the twenty undulating miles through Bruton and Somerton to Curry Rivel, achieving an almost 10min early arrival at Taunton. A rather tepid climb of Wellington bank preceded the next water stop but progress throughout kept strictly to the schedule and the arrivals at Exeter, Paignton and then Kingswear were all early.

A 10min late departure from Kingswear was converted into an early arrival at Exeter, but despite the irritating but apparently now permanent speed restriction at the Stonehill overbridge on the climb to Whiteball between MPs 181 and 180 which rather torpedoed the momentum developed beforehand, late arrival at Taunton was restricted to a couple of minutes. Throughout the day the locomotive behaved impeccably and its performance over a classic Western route was a suitable celebration of this significant landmark in the Society's and the locomotive's history.

31 July 2005
Bristol TM to Kingswear and return to Newton Abbot; 10 coaches; 126 miles; fine

The increasing lateness was such that the 'King' was terminated after it had arrived back at Yeovil for servicing and the train went directly to Victoria via Bournemouth diesel-hauled. The engine and support coach returned to Old Oak Common along the Berks & Hants.

9 June 2005
Victoria to Bristol TM via Reading and Westbury and return; 11 coaches; 257 miles; showers, then fine later
This was another good run outbound, apart from a moment climbing the bank to Savernake when the boiler primed. The return was marred by the unarrested wastage of water between Bristol and Bath, resulting in the level in the boiler getting very low and time wasted replenishing it. This altered the water demands further on so further delays ensued. The engine again performed faultlessly.

The first of the 'Torbay Express' series of the 2005 season, with three more to come, was an excellent opportunity for the locomotive. This is a perfect route for the passengers, with plenty of challenges for the locomotive and reasonable times to start and finish. Or so it was thought. The first run went like clockwork, with a lively engine and enthusiastic crews — until just east of Newton Abbot on the return, when a full brake application sent alarm bells ringing throughout the train.

A total air brake failure was diagnosed but, rather than attempt a repair on the open line, the proposal to proceed safely in vacuum brake mode to Exeter was made by the Traction Inspector but rejected by Network Rail. In the end, the train was diesel-towed from the rear back to Newton Abbot, locomotive and coach detached and the train taken onto Bristol by diesel. The engine then made its way to Exeter Riverside where the following day the fault — a leaking union — was diagnosed and repaired inside 10 minutes. No 6024 then returned to Bristol with a diesel pilot.

7 August 2005
Bristol TM to Kingswear and return; 10 coaches; 223 miles; Fine
Back with a vengeance, No 6024 bounced back from the previous weekend's disappointments with a top-drawer run with the 'Torbay Express'. A slight delay at Taunton on the outward run due to a late running service saw a cracking run up Wellington bank diving into Whiteball tunnel at a minimum of 46mph. The return journey was again sparkling, with line-speed running along the Teign Estuary and the seawall. An early departure from Exeter meant the pathing stop at Tiverton Loop was not needed and, despite the slack before the summit, Whiteball was topped at 44mph. Early arrival and departure from Taunton and Weston-super-Mare allowed the tour to arrive back in Bristol 17min early, concluding a comeback in fine fashion.

14 August 2005
Bristol TM to Kingswear and return; 10 coaches; 223 miles; Fine
The loco once again completed another good run with the 'Torbay Express', the outward run to the ex-GWR terminus at Kingswear being early. On the return journey a point's failure at Aller Junction put the train slightly behind and consequently the opportunity of an early departure from Exeter was not available. This meant the excellent performance out of Exeter had to be curtailed with a visit into Tiverton Loop for pathing. Once away though, a minimum of 46mph was achieved at the top of Whiteball with some sparkling running onto Taunton. A quick turn around reduced the deficit and with speeds again in the 70s along the Somerset levels the end of the run at Bristol was only a few minutes down on schedule.

28 August 2005 *(Table 24)*
Bristol TM to Kingswear and return; 10 coaches; 223 miles; Fine
What a fantastic day out to Kingswear with another great performance

Table 23: 2nd July 2005

LONDON PADDINGTON to KINGSWEAR, return to TAUNTON

Load: 11 coaches - 398 tons tare, 425 tons gross
Crew: *Drivers* A Hodges/D Clarke (to Westbury), M Hall (to Paignton)
Firemen D Clarke/A Hodges (to Westbury), R Binstead (to Paignton)
Traction Inspector C Kerswill (to Paignton)
Weather: Drizzle, mild, warmer and drier

Distance Miles/Ch.		Schedule	Actual	Speeds
	PADDINGTON	0	0.00	start
18.30	Slough	24.30	25.24	67
22.33	Taplow	--	28.54	71
24.13	Maidenhead	30.30	30.23	72
30.74	Twyford	40	36.13	69
35.72	READING	50.30	45.38	stop
8.65	Aldermaston	--	12.12	59
16.53	NEWBURY RACECOURSE	30.30	24.35	stop
3.38	Hamstead Crossing	--	12.15	54
5.67	Kintbury	--	14.50	57
8.72	Hungerford	--	18.09	54
13.62	Bedwyn	19	23.28	56
17.37	*Savernake summit*	--	27.48	45
26.22	Woodborough	30	36.25	70
28.48	Patney	--	38.22	70
35.35	*Lavington*	38	43.57	70
42.77	WESTBURY	49	53.03	stop
5.60	FROME	15	13.56	stop
5.29	*East Somerset Jn.*	--	12.42	46
7.08	*Brewham summit*	--	14.59	44
10.45	Bruton	--	18.07	78
14.01	Castle Cary	19	20.52	71
24.30	Somerton	--	30.12	72
29.46	Curry Rivel Jn.	--	34.23	76
37.04	Cogload Jn.	54	42.28	22 check
41.46	TAUNTON	61	51.35	stop
4.43	*Bradford Crossing*	--	7.54	49
10.01	*Whiteball tunnel (East)*	--	15.54	29
10.68	*MP 174 Whiteball Summit*	--	17.37	31
14.16	Tiverton Parkway	20	21.44	32
15.78	TIVERTON DOWN LOOP	25	26.14	stop
0.00	TIVERTON DOWN LOOP	0	0.00	start
6.31	*Hele & Bradninch*	--	9.20	66
11.06	*Stoke Canon*	--	13.28	72
14.62	EXETER St. DAVIDS	20	18.43	stop
6.58	*Powderham Crossing*	--	8.42	66
10.42	Dawlish Warren	13	12.12 *sigs*	54
15.01	Teignmouth	--	21.15	48
20.13	Newton Abbot	29	27.48 *sigs*	21
28.20	PAIGNTON	52	49.05	stop
6.52	KINGSWEAR	35	31.33	stop
0.00	KINGSWEAR	0	0.00	start
6.52	PAIGNTON	30	32.13	stop
7.03	*MP 215 Aller Jn.*	--	13.18	37
8.07	Newton Abbot	21	14.57	45
13.19	Teignmouth	--	20.30	58
17.55	Dawlish Warren	32	25.03	61
21.42	*Powderham Crossing*	--	28.33	69
26.60	*City Basin Jn.*	--	33.10	58
28.20	EXETER St. DAVIDS	46	37.04	stop
3.56	*Stoke Canon*	--	7.26	52
14.62	Tiverton Parkway	19	21.34	55
19.72	*MP 174 Whiteball Summit*	--	25.23	50
25.72	*MP 168*	--	30.44	70
26.17	*Bradford Crossing*	--	31.01	70
30.60	TAUNTON	34	36.31	stop

PAIGNTON to BRISTOL TEMPLE MEADS				
Load:	10 coaches - 365 tons tare, 395 tons gross			
Crew:	Driver T. Rees			
	Fireman F Lewis			
	Traction Inspector G Jones			
	Weather: Dry, fine			
Distance		**Schedule**	**Actual**	**Speeds**
Miles/Ch.	PAIGNTON	0	0.00	start
2.13	Torquay	--	5.33	36
5.73	Kingskerswell	--	13.27	46
8.07	Newton Abbot	25	14.31	50
13.19	Teignmouth	--	19.45	61
17.58	Dawlish Warren	38	24.06	63
23.41	Exminster	--	29.23	68
28.20	EXETER St. DAVIDS	51	36.20	stop
1.20	Cowley Bridge Jn.	--	3.27	41
6.31	Hele & Bradninch	--	10.57	65
9.72	MP 184	--	12.22	65
14.78	TIVERTON UP LOOP	21	20.38	stop
1.78	Tiverton Parkway	5	3.23	47
5.34	MP 174 Whiteball Summit	--	7.19	52
6.01	Whiteball tunnel (East)	--	7.34	65
7.34	MP 172	--	9.10	78/81
9.14	Wellington	--	10.37	76
11.88	Bradford Crossing	--	12.32	77
14.34	MP 165	--	14.45	66
16.23	TAUNTON	21	17.54	stop
4.88	Cogload Jn.	7	7.20	52
11.64	Bridgwater	12	13.21	71
17.86	Highbridge	19	18.39	70/72
25.07	Uphill Jn.	27	25.51	45
26.75	WESTON-SUPER-MARE	31	29.45	stop
2.28	Worle Jn.	5	6.12	39
7.11	Yatton	--	11.01	68
11.06	Nailsea and Backwell	--	14.29	68
13.65	Flax Bourton Tunnel	--	16.42	66/70
17.24	Parson St	--	20.32	43
19.08	BRISTOL TEMPLE MEADS	29	26.50	stop

hauling the 'Torbay Express'! The outward run was slightly marred by an unscheduled stop at Flax Bourton owing to the new firebox deflector plate falling into the firebox. There was no sign of it when the loco was serviced at Paignton! The return journey was simply stunning, with the Newport crew of Driver Tom Rees, Fireman Fred Lewis and Trainee Fireman Chris Rees under the expert eye of Traction Inspector Gareth Jones making the loco run like a dream. Torre bank was dismissed with ease and the seawall section was taken at a canter. Early away from Exeter, mile after mile was taken in the mid-60s on the rising grades to a pathing stop at Tiverton Loop. Once away though, the climb to Whiteball summit was fabulous, the loco accelerating all the way to the top with a minimum of 51.5mph being achieved before diving into the tunnel and onto Taunton. A quick servicing stop was followed by more stunning running and Bristol Temple Meads was reached some 27min early. A superb run!

4 September 2005

Bristol TM to Kingswear and return; 10 coaches; 223 miles; fine
This run also went like clockwork, until the run up to Churston in the hands of the P&DSR crew coincided with a tropical storm and the loco stalled on the bank. Having exhausted the sand-boxes, delicate nursing of the locomotive was called for and combined with hand-sanding, the engine and train struggled to the top. To avoid too much time being curtailed at Kingswear and to allow sufficient time for the engine to be serviced and turned the return run was rescheduled. Apart from another bout of priming, at Torre, another fine run returned the train safely to Bristol.

7 September 2005

Taunton to Stratford-upon-Avon via Bristol TM and Oxford, return to Bristol TM; 12 coaches; 342 miles; fine
This was a complicated operation with some substantial logistical challenges because of the distances involved, an over-optimistic schedule throughout and the number of stops for picking up and setting down. The load alone was enough cause to doubt that timings could be maintained. The many stops ensured that. The stock with the locomotive on the rear running tender-first was hauled by diesel to Taunton. Then, after the start, with stops at Bridgwater, Yatton and Nailsea before Bristol, the 'King' did its best to maintain time. Some unimpressive work followed the departure from Bristol but matters livened up either side of the Swindon water-stop and onto Banbury, Warwick and into Stratford, the schedule was just about kept under control, with a late arrival of only five minutes.

Turning and servicing at the halfway point was not easy because the movement involved marshalling the stock as well as the run to Dorridge and back to the triangle at Hatton. All this had to be threaded through the service-train schedule and with Stratford station being busier than ever, it proved impossible to do all that was needed in the time allowed. Departure on the return was 20min late. Despite this, a vigorous attack was made on the climb to Fosse Road and the engine was given its head on the largely level stretch after Fenny Compton before the run down to Banbury. Watering was accomplished quickly at Banbury, but the schedule was increasingly under pressure and, at the next stop at Oxford, was irretrievable. Filling up with water would save time at the next water-stop at Challow, but before then, the completely unexpected happened with the engine being driven through a red signal at Didcot North junction. Here the whole job came to a standstill, resulting in the end of the steam-hauled work with a delay of a couple of hours. The driver having been immediately suspended the operation was paralysed until eventually the fireman was permitted to collect a Class 66 from the EWS Didcot depot and pilot the train back to Bristol where the engine and coach detached.

10 September 2005

Bristol TM to Birmingham SH via Severn Tunnel, Hereford and Worcester; nine coaches; 133 miles; dry, then rain, then dry
This run was sponsored by the Society to relocate the engine back at its facilities at the Tyseley Locomotive Works for its first 12-month exam of its current boiler ticket. In deteriorating weather conditions the engine produced some good work on the heavy climbs of Horfield, out of the

18 December 2005 — In low winter sunshine a special from Paddington to Stratford-upon-Avon threads its way through the London suburbs at Park Royal.
Mike Tyack

Severn tunnel, Llanvihangel and Old Hill that feature on the route, including the third fastest ever ascent of Old Hill bank, following the first and second places also held by the locomotive, created in March 2002.

18 December 2005

Paddington to Stratford Upon Avon via High Wycombe, and return; 10 coaches; 238 miles; cold, fine

After some much-needed 'down-time' to fix a number of things which required attention after an extremely busy season, the locomotive moved to London for a couple of rail-tours. In the event one was postponed so this was the one remaining. Through no fault of the locomotive the start was not auspicious. In use the previous day and having arrived back late, the coaching stock had been caught up in an overnight engineering possession and had not returned to Old Oak Common for servicing. When it eventually arrived the 'King' was hooked on and departure from Paddington was two hours late. Unable to top up with water during this period and with regular speed restrictions imposed between High Wycombe meant that the running was steady rather than lively to Banbury. Thereafter, greater energy was evident but there was no net gain on the delay. With the need to service and turn no time could be saved at Stratford. On the whole the return was livelier and arrival in Paddington was about 100min late, but with no time lost due to the locomotive.

The locomotive completed 2005 competently and played its part with its habitual energy. Although the year ended on a rather low-key note, this was relative to what had proved to be an exhilarating and impressive year. The 'Torbay Expresses' never had a dull moment. These were most enjoyable days out for the passengers as well as the loco and her crew members. Sunny days on the English Riviera! Each train was sold out and it was interesting to note that most passengers were not enthusiasts, but ordinary members of the public who wanted to enjoy a good old-fashioned excursion to the seaside. Other than the well-documented blip with the air pipe fracture on the first run, all went smoothly and the loco's reputation was enhanced even further as a strong, reliable performer.

The engine had in fact completed well over 5,000 interesting miles on the main line in the year (which included its three months off) and apart from the air system producing a couple of headaches it had produced an impeccable record for reliability.

Conclusion

Many thanks are offered to you, the readers of this book. We trust you have enjoyed it and hopefully it will have evoked and prompted a range of feelings and thoughts; hours of enjoyment; happy recollections of exciting times on the main line with the 'King'; a permanent record of those times; admiration for the locomotive itself and empathy for those who look after it; respect for those who stick their necks out and promote main-line steam rail-tours; admiration for the skill of those who have taken the pictures; encouragement to continue to support the Society and the activities of *King Edward I* by travelling with it on its work on the main line; and perhaps a spur to you to join us in the 6024 Society.

Since 1973 the Society and its locomotive have benefited from assistance of every variety — including direct involvement, donations, grants and hospitality — from many hundreds of individuals and organisations. Therefore, we should not forget to thank firstly all the past and present members of the 6024 Preservation Society Ltd, who, each in their own way, have made a crucial contribution to the continued life of *King Edward I*. Additional thanks must also go to all the active volunteers, who, since 1990, have devoted so much of their leisure time to the upkeep and operation of the locomotive and all its associated activities.

Thanks must go to all the many hundreds of passengers who have paid to travel on 'King'-hauled charters — especially those with thousands of 6024 'Rail Miles' on the clock! Without them there would be no steam on the main line; it is that simple.

Thanks must go to the rail-tour promoters and their predecessors who, since 1990, have contracted the Society to provide the locomotive for main-line charter-work and who have been the Society's principal clients: the *Bristol Evening Post,* Kingfisher Railtours, Past Time Rail, Pathfinder Tours, Steam Dreams, Steamy Affairs, the Railway Touring Company and Vintage Trains; also thanks must go to the number of other organisations who have promoted the occasional rail-tour using No 6024. Thanks also go to the specialist national press and to video film-makers for their coverage of steam in general and of No 6024 in particular.

Also special thanks must go to the footplate crews of the former British Rail and past and present crews of English, Welsh & Scottish Railways, Fragonset Merlin Rail and West Coast Railways; also to the authorities within the former British Rail and Railtrack and to those currently within Network Rail, who have supported and facilitated steam on the main line.

Thanks also are due to all the staff of the Birmingham Railway Museum and Tyseley Locomotive Works, the Bodmin & Wenford Railway, the former Bulmers Railway Centre in Hereford, the Crewe Heritage Centre, the Great Western Society at Didcot, the National

Mike Spencer

Railway Museum, the Paignton & Dartmouth Steam Railway, the Severn Valley Railway, the Southall Steam Centre, the Watercress Line (Mid Hants Railway), the West Somerset Railway and the Yeovil Railway Centre; also to the staff of the motive power depots at Aylesbury, Bescot, Bounds Green, Bristol's Bath Road, Barton Hill and St Philips Marsh, Cardiff Canton, Carlisle Upperby, Exeter Riverside, Gloucester, Newport Godfrey Road, Norwich, Old Oak Common, Peterborough, Plymouth Laira, St Blazey, Stewarts Lane, Swansea Landore and Worcester; and also to all the many contractors and suppliers who have assisted the Society in keeping its 75-year-old pride and joy in top condition.

Finally, thanks again to the photographers — please continue to produce fabulous images of the locomotive.

All profits from the sales of this book will be devoted to the upkeep and operation of *King Edward I* so it can continue to work on the main line for as long as main-line steam continues to have a future.